Live Life!
Be Young,
Black and Successful

By
Quincy Benton

www.quincybenton.com

2005 by Live Life! Publishing

All products mentioned in this book are trademarks of their respective companies.

Live Life! Publishing and colophon are
registered trademarks of **Live Life! Publishing**, Inc.

Library of Congress Cataloging-in-Publication Data
Benton, Quincy *Live Life! Be Young, Black and Successful* / Quincy Benton.
Includes bibliographical references.
ISBN   0-9729812-1-5

Printed in the United States of America

To Contact Quincy Benton

Visit **www.quincybenton.com** to purchase copies of the book. Quantity discounts are available. Also, visit the site to contact Quincy Benton directly and to find up-to-date information on "Q's Car," the young African Americans interviewed for the book, and the latest developments at Live Life! Publishing.

How to order books

Contact: Independent Publishers Group, Inc.
814 North Franklin Street • Chicago, Illinois 60610
1.800.888.4741 • orders@ipgbook.com

Visit us online at **www.quincybenton.com**

Foreword

How should we as young, African-Americans live our lives? And, how should we live our lives as God has designed? These are two vitally important questions that at some point during your adult life you will have to answer. How you answer these questions will ultimately decide whether you will live a life full of happiness, wellness, and love or a life riddled with depression, sickness, and hate. Whatever life you choose to live, know that it is *Your choice!* *Your choice* to choose good over bad, wealth over poverty, or sickness over health. *Your choice* to deal in the dastardly deeds of the world or to grow in the eternal goodness of God. Will you choose to *Live Life!* or Live Death??? My hope is that you will choose to *Live Life!* That you will choose to *Live Life!* with the hope, love, peace, health, ambition and wealth that God has entitled your life. That you will choose to Denounce Death and the devilish tools of hate, lust, greed, and deceit. *Choose Life! Live Life! Be Life! Give Life!* And know by doing so, you are choosing to *Live Life!* with the success that God has intended. Join me in my journey to Empower our Lives, Better our Lives, and Live our Lives to Be Young, Black and Successful!

Table of Contents

Introduction..1

What is Success? 2

The Style: Learning the Techniques to be Young, Black and Successful

Taking The Right Steps 15

How Did They Do It? 17

Are Successful Young, African-Americans Naturally More Gifted? 17

The Canvas: Creating the Mindset for Young, Black Success

Developing The Mindset To Be Young, Black and Successful 20

Self-Actualization...22

Other Keys To Developing The Success Mindset...23

Optimize Your Opportunity...25

Failing To Optimize Your Opportunity..26

Lots Of Ideas, Lots Of Energy, No Focus – Bad Combination.........................28

Discipline Your Mind To Produce the Results You Desire................................30

The Law Of Relationships..32

Coming Out Of "I" To Embrace "We"..33

Anything And Everything Is Possible..35

All Eyes On Me..37

Maintaining Significant Increases..39

Let The Truth Be Told About The Dollar...40

The Easel: Supporting the Canvas of Young, Black Success

Angels On Earth...45

The Importance Of Family..47

Good Timing..49

Is Knowledge Power?...51

Counting Blessings..53

How Do You Count Blessings?..55

The Tools: Painting the Picture for Young, Black Success

You Are What You Do!..58

Raising The Standard..60

Step Out Of The Box..61

The Price Of Success..66

So What You Gonna Do?..68

Not Allowing Your Minimums to be Your Maximums..69

Don't Start What You Can't Finish..72

Get Out And Make It Happen..73

Get And Stay Married..75

Controlling Careless Consumption..77

Are You Willing To Bear The Burden?..81

The Power Of Galvanizing..86

The Power Of Production..89

Other Keys To Mastering The Power Of Production..92

Champions Never Take The Easy Way Out – Pay the Price..94

The Inspiration: Bringing Forth What's Within to Create Young, Black Success

Listen To Your Spirit..98

Value Versus Dollars..101

The Mathematics Of Life..104

The Masterpiece: Past, Present, You are the Future!

We Have the Power!..109

Special Thanks

Bibliography

Live Life!
Be Young,
Black and Successful

By
Quincy Benton

www.quincybenton.com

Introduction

As a young African-American man, I know first hand how desperately young brothers and sisters want to be successful. For years, I have watched and listened to the increasing number of visual and auditory images that appear on television, radio, and in print media showcasing how African-Americans are attaining success and creating lives people never imagined.

I have also spent hours talking to young brothers and sisters about the new influx of visibly successful young, African-Americans emerging on the American landscape. People like Master P – President and CEO of No Limit Records; Laila Ali – professional boxer; and tennis greats Venus and Serena Williams have and continue to be at the center of our discussions about African- Americans and their achievement of success. Although the accomplishments of these individuals and the accomplishments of other young, African-Americans with well-publicized stories of success are best known, this does not mean that all successes are or have to be achieved at this level. Success comes in all shapes, sizes, and formats. True beauty, insight, and peace of mind comes to those who study and appreciate the kaleidoscope of noteworthy accomplishments achieved by all African-Americans. By exposing ourselves to all our stories of success, we confirm the belief that you do not have to own a multi-media conglomerate, make millions of dollars, or set world records in order to be considered successful. And through this process of enlightenment, we destroy the taboo that an individual has to sell their soul to accomplish visible achievements or to accumulate large sums of money.

Through the more than forty interviews that I have conducted with the successful, young, African- Americans you will soon read about representing a variety of professions, beliefs, and backgrounds, I have discovered that we (young, African- Americans) have an assortment of beliefs about success. Although our backgrounds are different, success-oriented African-Americans all agree that success is more than just money or material possessions. This consensus, however, does not put an end to the curiosities that people have surrounding individuals who have achieved certain types of successes. Regardless of the people with whom I've talked or what the discussion is about, each conversation always seems to end with the same probing questions or thoughts about success: How did he or she do it? And, more important, how can I do that myself?

What is Success?

I think people get caught up thinking that success is just about making a million dollars. That's not what it's all about. Success is about bettering yourself and being able to stay on top of your game. That's what a lot of people don't understand about successful people. Successful people constantly better themselves and improve their ability to survive in this world. Whether they do it in business, corporate America, or the streets – success can be achieved.

–Master P
Founder and CEO
No Limit Records

For me, I think ignoring other people has been very important because other people will always tell you what you need to do in your life while doing nothing in theirs. It's like taking financial advice from someone who is broke – I'm not doing that because obviously if you knew what you were talking about you'd be rich. You need to do the things you're trying to tell me I need to do. What I have found to be important is looking at that person and looking at what they've accomplished in their lives, not even in terms of tangible successes, because success is not always measured in something tangible. But, it's how they live their lives and the people they have in their lives and how they treat those people before I put any merit into what they're saying. Because I should know better than anybody what's good for me. I can take advice and suggestions. But, I'm not going to apply any of that stuff unless I think it works for me. So, you really have to look at the source. Look at the source - whoever is telling you something, whoever is asking you to do something. Especially if it's something that challenges what you think is the right thing for you in your heart. To really question the source.

–Ananda Lewis
Television Personality

What is Success?

Really, I don't have a formula for my own success other than God's grace. I know a lot of people who are much smarter, more talented, more committed and better read than I am. But, I was given the break for a blessing. When you look at all the things that have happened in my life, I have every reason why I shouldn't be where I am this early. The fact that I flunked the eleventh grade. The fact that I have a G.E.D. The fact that I got into Morehouse (College) on probation. The fact that I had a child out of wedlock. All of the things that add up to explain why I shouldn't be pastor of The Empowerment Temple.

–Rev. Jamal Harrison-Bryant
Pastor, The Empowerment Temple
Baltimore, Maryland

In order to be successful, you first have to start with your dream – look for something that you can get completely passionate about. Next, you have to have faith (in God) that you can make your dream reality. Then, seek the knowledge. Finally, combine these elements with dedication and discipline, and you will be prepared for your opportunity when it comes.

–Mara Brock-Akil
Television Producer
Girlfriends

What is Success?

My definition of success is being able to take care of yourself and your family comfortably while reaching your fullest potential. I think that God has given every individual on this Earth talent. And it is up to each individual to be proactive in showcasing that talent. In your attempt to reach your fullest potential, you will discover that you will touch numerous lives. You will also have gained and achieved so many things in life that when you look back upon your journey – you will be very satisfied.

–Maurice Evans,
Professional Basketball Player

One thing you have to be is dedicated. You have to be dedicated to what you are doing and you have to set goals for yourself. Once you do that, you cannot look back. You have to put forth your best effort in whatever it is that you do. I always stress that the most important thing you can do is to listen to your parents and to the people who are there to guide you. They are there to lead you in the right direction. One big thing I would say to any child is the key to success is listening.

–Michael Vick
Professional Football Player

What is Success?

Success shouldn't be determined on your material value. There are a lot of successful people in this world who are not wealthy. Success should be determined on how much of a positive impact you've had on your fellow man. When you've been blessed with talents, whether they are physical or mental talents, I think that it's extremely important for you to share those talents with others. We were put on this Earth to help each other out. Whether we want to believe it or not, we need each other. We do. We were put on this Earth because we need each other. You need the mailman. You need the gas station attendant. We all need each other for something. So, why try to bring each other down? Always try to encourage people and go through each and everyday making a concerted effort to give somebody something positive. And it doesn't have to be material things. You can give somebody words of encouragement. You can give somebody your smile. You can uplift their day with words and just positive energy. I think it's extremely important to take that approach. I look at it as a cycle. It's a cycle that runs through the world: whatever you put out eventually comes back to you. If you're putting out good energy – you're making people happy, you're making people feel good – then you are going to be happy. You're going to feel good. You are going to get that back. And that's just how the world works. If you're constantly making a concerted effort to hurt people, then it's going to catch up to you. I'm sure you're familiar with the word karma. Overall, the most important thing is to restructure your life and to live it the best way that you can. Don't just live it for yourself. But, live it to encourage and to help others. And that's success.

–Alonzo Mourning
Professional Basketball Player

I think a big part of being successful is knowing who you are and what you stand for because that's your foundation. There will be times when other people will have opinions and try to sway you one way or the other. And you'll just be moving in all these different directions and not in the direction that you want to go. So, that's the first thing that you have to know is who you are and what you stand for and what you want to do. I think a lot of that has to do with having a relationship with God. And from there, you can do anything you want. As long as you know who you are and you're doing what you want to do and you're happy, in life, I think that you are a successful person.

–Laila Ali
Professional Boxer

What is Success?

My definition of success is to feel like I've made a difference. To know that I've made a difference in a child's life, or made a difference in an industry, or made a difference in an individual's life here at the company, or made a difference in my own life by continuing to evolve and do better. The process of constant and never-ending improvement is about the journey of success. If you're constantly improving and evolving, then ultimately the results will take care of themselves. If you focus on simple results, you're going to be disappointed day in and day out. But, if you focus on being the best that you can be and build on that everyday, then you can say that I was successful at being better (every situation – everyday) then I'll take what God is going to give me. And that's how I live my life. I do the best that I can everyday and then I accept what the Good Lord is going to give me. Regardless of what we like to say, there are certain things that we cannot control. The thing that I can control is myself and to be the best. That's what success is for me.

–Alan F. Daniels
Former Founder, Chairman and CEO RealEstate.com

The first component of success is knowing that you deserve to be successful and that you have everything that you need to make it happen. So many young people don't realize that just given what they have to have to survive on a daily basis gives them the components that they need to be successful. But, it starts with knowing who you are and knowing what you want. It starts with being determined. It starts with being dynamic and always knowing that you have to be better than your counterparts. You have to be faster. You have to be more intelligent. You have to be a better crisis manager. You have to be better. And then know that when you are, nobody can ever take that from you because people will try that. They'll try to get you to think that you're not as good as you think you are.
They'll try to tell you that being assertive and being confident and being ambitious translates into having an attitude. They'll try to tell you that – if you let them. But, you can't let them. You have to be driven by what you know to be true inside. And so much of that comes from being grounded in a strong Faith. You gotta know from whence you came. You gotta know whose shoulders you're standing on. You gotta know whose steps you're climbing. You gotta know who is really in charge. If you have all these things and you're able to focus and you know where you're going, then you're going to be successful. Who is there other than yourself to stop you? We have glass ceilings. We have the great racial divide. But, you can always change your course. Nobody can ever tell you what your pinnacle is. And if you get to a certain place and you're dealing with the glass ceiling, then you change your course. You look at what is really of value in your life and what is really important.

–Elise Durham
Media Relations Professional

What is Success?

My definition of success is living my life how I want to live my life. And that, a lot of times is easier said than done. When I attended Spelman (College), I was a General Motors Scholar, which means that after graduation I was guaranteed a job at General Motors. But, I knew that I wanted to be an entertainer - I wasn't happy in the corporate environment. Now, that's just me. Some people are happy there. So, what did I do? I moved into a really, really cheap apartment. I ate Ramen noodles everyday for three months while hanging out in one dance studio trying to learn the style of dance that Atlanta was into. I stayed at this dance studio constantly. I got the vibe – I got the feeling. I kept going on audition after audition. My family didn't understand why I would give up a $60K a year job to be a starving artist. Although I was a starving artist, I was happy. I really felt like had I gone into corporate America I would have developed an ulcer from being stressed out not doing what I wanted to do. I believed that if I did what made me happy I would be provided for - money would come, and I would be taken care of. Eventually, I went through the starving artist thing and then it got to the point where I couldn't believe people were paying me to dance and to entertain. Because it's my passion – it's what I love. And that comes across in my work. When you enjoy what you're doing, it shows – and you will be rewarded for that. That's my definition of success.

–Sharmell Sullivan
World Wrestling Entertainment Smackdown! Superstar

I think success is when you can do what you do professionally without having to give up any of your soul or who you are in the process. There are a lot of successful people in this business, but I think there are very few people that are *truly* successful. Many have cut a part of themselves out of them. And you can see it. No matter how rich, no matter how whatever they are, they're not the same people that they used to be. I feel fortunate because I haven't had to cut out my soul - that belongs to me. That doesn't belong to Hollywood. "What is it for man to gain the world, if he loses his soul?" as the saying goes. That's my thing. The moment I feel like I'm giving up my soul, then I'm not successful.

–John Singleton
Movie Producer

What is Success?

Success is three things. It's achieving your goals while fulfilling your purpose and remaining true to yourself. First, goals apply to any and everything. Success is not a professional thing. Success is not a personal thing. It's a self-defined, life-long thing. Everybody has to define success for themselves. Nine times out of ten, our definition of success is not the same as the next person. For example, you may see somebody walking in the snow and say he/she is not successful because they don't have a car or because they have to ride the bus. But, that person might be just as happy and feel that he/she is successful because they are reaching their goals. Second, I think that everybody is here for a reason. And, hopefully at some point we figure what that reason is. So, you're achieving your goals while fulfilling your purpose. One of my primary purposes here is to educate people. I've been blessed with the gift of understanding – helping people sort through their personal and/or professional relationships. My ability to understand and help people better understand their circumstances is what I'm here to do while remaining true to myself, which brings me to the third component – remaining true to yourself. Again, when I'm on my time I do what I want. The game don't change me. I've chosen this time to play the corporate game. But, it does not change the person I am. I'm a 28 year-old, hip-hop head with my Yankee cap on backwards during the weekend. And, I'm fine like that. By other people's definition, that's not how I should be based upon my position and status in corporate America. But, it's who I am. And, I don't see anything wrong with that. So that's success. It's fulfilling your purpose, reaching your goals, while remaining true.

–Malcolm K. Berkley
Public Relations Professional

A successful person is someone who is able to use his or her God-given talents. And each of us is given a talent. The adventure is finding what that talent is. Once you find out what your talent is, success comes when you're able to use it on your own terms, use it well and when you're able to give it back. When I was growing up, I thought success was 'I'm gonna be rich or I'm gonna do this.' As I've gotten older, I realize that you don't necessarily have to be rich to be successful. Although the more successful you get, the richer you'll become.

–Tiffany K. Cochran
11Alive News Anchor
WXIA-TV Atlanta

What is Success?

I consider success to be both personal and professional. One of the ways I measure personal success is by happiness and being content. And then I measure professional success by the ability to set goals and achieve them; satisfaction with your work and your accomplishments, having the existence of many opportunities; and by comparsion of your progress among your peers. However, success is different for everybody. And it depends a lot on your nature. I am an analytical person who is inquistive. I like to ask a lot of questions and really understand the meat of what it is that I am working on. But, I am also willing to take risks and try some adventurous paths. And I try to make decisions that provide me many opportunities. Ever since I was a child, I've had an interest in astronomy. But, I decided to major in engineering because I likedit and because I thought that I had more opportunities as an engineer. I studied mechanical engineering in undergraduate school knowing that I could always fall backon building cars, bridges, or other practical kinds of things. I then went on to studyaerospace engineering in graduate school. Although I wanted to be astronaut and knew that's what I really wanted to do, I also knew that if the industry was not hiring or for some reason things were not goingwell, I could fall back on the mechanical engineering. So, I always tried to choose the path that would give me the most opportunities. I think for me that has been critical to being successful.

–Stephanie Wilson
Astronaut
National Aeronautics and Space Administration (NASA)

I define success as enjoying what I'm doing while having no idea that I am doing things that people look at and are really fascinated by, or laugh at and think are great. I enjoy what I'm doing so much that I don't think about whether people are going to like it or whether they think I'm talented. I just do it because I enjoy it and have a great time doing it. I go with the script and think about what I am going to bring to it and how I can make it as silly and as fun as possible. And then I hope for accolades after that. But, I never know. So, I don't harp on that. I learned from Jim Henson and Frank Oz (creators of Sesame Street) to just be silly – to just have a good time. And hopefully if it makes you laugh - everybody else will. But, I don't know. I have no idea. So, I don't worry about it."

–Kevin Clash
Puppeteer/Voice
Sesame Street's *Elmo*

What is Success?

Success is discovering the true meaning of the word. First, understand that you can't measure success by things that are tangible. You measure success by things that are intangible - qualities and virtues like being sane, understanding love, appreciating your forefathers, knowing yourself, meeting challenges before they meet you, having compassion for other people, and sharing blessings. Second, success is also reaching a point of knowing that if you died tomorrow you would be satisfied with the way you've lived your life. There are too many stories of people who have "sold their souls" losing their sense of integrity and self-worth in the pursuit of success. And last, success is coming to the realization that you can't always "make" success happen. Sometimes you have to "let" it happen. Accepting these truths, you will experience  the success of having a lifestyle that is healthy and days that start off with hope for a better tomorrow.

–Justin Clay
Founder and CEO
The Renality Foundation For Kidney Disease

My perspective about money is totally different than most of my peers. I don't place as high a value on money as they do. Many of my friends are simply afraid to lose. As a result, they are limited in what they are willing to do because they're always thinking that they'll go broke if it doesn't work. That doesn't worry me. If I go broke, I'll just pick myself up and start all over again. Be willing to take the risk! My willingness to take the risk combined with my work ethic has separated me from the rest.

–Komichel Johnson
Co-founder and Partner
JLW Development, LLC

What is Success?

To be phenomenally successful, you have to be selfish to a certain extent. I believe Michael Jordan said it best when he was asked at the end of his career what were his plans after leaving basketball. Michael stated that he was going to spend more time at home with his family because he had taken so much away by doing and being who he was. Michael realized that he had to be that way in order to achieve the things he has achieved. From a political perspective, people tend to believe that it's not a good thing to be selfish. However, I have yet to discover individuals who have achieved large scales of success do so by being altruistic or considering other people's aspirations over their own. These individuals had to have the focus and the willingness to put everything on the side in order to do it. And, it takes a degree of selfishness.

–Edward S. Brown,
President and CEO
Edward S. Brown International, Inc.

There are things that I say to myself to keep me uplifted. It's rare that I'm being uplifted by somebody else. Actually, when it's time for me to be uplifted by somebody, I end up uplifting them. What keeps my spirit positive is that I appreciate all things in life. And that's one thing a lot of us don't do. We don't take the time to appreciate what we have. And when I start thinking about 'Well, I don't have this or I don't have that, or look at my life...' I realize that your life dictates your future. Yesterday is history. Today is the gift. And, my future is untold. And that's how I look at it. I can't dwell on yesterday because it's gone – it's forgotten. Today is going to be over in a couple of hours. So with my future, I keep pressing forward and saying, 'It's not how I started this race, it's how I finished.' Even when it seems like the whole world is falling around me, I always remember someone else is going through something similar or worse. So, I've learned how to appreciate my life. Now, that's success to me.

–Angela M. Lewis
Motivational Strength Leader

What is Success?

Success is attained when a person identifies a goal, sets in place a plan, and acts tirelessly towards the fulfillment of that goal. The mistake that most people make is only measuring their success by the outcome of their endeavors. They are wrong. If that were the case, Herman Melville, author of *Moby Dick*, was a failure. His book did not become a classic until after his death. So, remember that success lies in the doing. The man or woman who persistently moves forward toward their dream, armed with a blueprint and the conviction to pursue it to the end, will achieve success.

–Wes Hall, Motivational
Speaker/Author
You Are The Money

I think there are different paths down the road to success, but all of them require some vested effort. Although there's something to be said for being in the right place at the right time, you can't always control that. You still have to have what it takes. For example, imagine you were an aspiring singer that didn't have any connections in the music industry. One day, you were walking down the street and it just so happened that the head of artist development at a major record label overheard you singing. That would be cool! But, if you were no good, that person would just walk by. That's being in the right place at the right time. However, the question would become - do you have what it takes, in terms of skills, to win this person over? Skill only comes from practice and hard work. Nobody is so good at something that they can't get better somehow.

–Ayinde Jean-Baptiste
12-year-old speaker at the Million Man March

What is Success?

Success comes down to service. When I say "service", I don't necessarily mean going down to a homeless shelter. That's great, but what I am really saying is being of service in your everyday life. Saying a kind word to somebody who needs it - that's service. Being that bright light for somebody surrounded by gloom – that's service. Being that source of peace for someone in the midst of conflict - that's service. Your service is your lifestyle. I don't think we need to just stand on corners with books in our hands. We just need to live. Live life; that's it!

–Jonathan Lee Iverson
First African-American Ringmaster
Ringling Brothers and Barnum & Bailey Circus

Success to me means achieving your goals – at least trying to. I'm not going to sit up here and say that success IS achieving your goals. Because as long as you're trying, and you're trying to push, and you're staying focused, then I feel like that's success. Like me, I haven't made it to all the places that I want to be yet. I haven't made it to half of them. But, I feel like I have success because I'm trying. I haven't given up yet. Although, people seem to think I did.

–Tiffany Richardson,
*America's Next
Top Model4* Finalist

13

The Style: Learning the Techniques to be Young, Black and Successful

Taking The Right Steps

People who are unfamiliar with what it takes to be successful tend to believe there are secret passageways or secret societies that automatically open the doors to achievement. Their theories are muddied by thoughts that all successful men and women have known the "right people," have been blessed with the "right looks," or have come from the "right families." While these views do explain certain types of successes, they definitely do not account for all. It appears that the people who buy into these notions typically come from environments where successful individuals with success-oriented mindsets are hard to find.

Many people can clearly tell you what they want in life (i.e. drive luxury cars, own their own businesses, become more spiritually enlightened, make a million dollars by the age of thirty, and etc.). However, when you ask these same individuals how and when they are going to achieve their goals, their answers become quite vague – even illogical. For example, I have talked with high school counselors who have told me stories of students who shared with them their grand plans to become doctors or lawyers. However, when these advisors took the time to ask these students when they were going to study for or were planning to take the Scholastic Aptitude Test (SAT) or the American College Testing Assessment (ACT), many replied that they were not prepared and/or were not scheduled to take one of these essential exams. The notion of becoming a doctor or lawyer without taking or preparing to take the SAT or ACT clearly demonstrates the lack of understanding held by certain individuals concerning the steps needed to accomplish specific goals.

First, every practicing doctor or lawyer knows that in order to enter their profession, a person has to achieve the minimum score on the SAT or ACT needed for entrance into the college of their choosing. Second, one must be accepted into that college and be successful academically in order to graduate. But, the process does not stop there. Next, the future doctor or lawyer must start the admissions process again in order to gain acceptance into a medical or law school. Upon completion of the coursework, the medical student must complete a residency for licensure and the law student must pass the bar exam. It is only after completing these steps (a process that takes anywhere from six to ten years upon graduating from high school) will the individual become a doctor or lawyer.

Unfortunately, many students do not have a detailed understanding of the steps required to enter a profession. Consequently, as with the college admissions process, the lack of understanding about the process of achieving specific goals in life (like becoming a doctor or lawyer) prevents many from accumulating the levels of success that they truly desire. Perhaps the root of this ignorance stems from a lack of knowledge. After all, parents cannot teach their children the process of achieving goals if they, in fact, have not been taught themselves.

In an Ebony magazine interview with multi-platinum recording artist, Erykah Badu, the Grammy award-winning artist revealed her awareness of the steps required for success. When asked about her plans for raising her son Seven, Badu replied, "We want to give him the hard truths at the beginning of life, so he won't have to be like me and (his) daddy, unlearning a bunch of crap that messed us up as human beings." She went on to say, "We intend to give Seven the straight truth about life with no sugar-coating, no fairy tales. That way he can go ahead and start being the beautiful person that he is..." From her comments, it is evident that Badu is has already begun mapping out her plans for Seven's future.

While Badu's comments might seem insignificant in the context of her recording career, they give tremendous insight into her strategy for ensuring the success of her son. She understands that you have to plan! Case in point: If you were preparing for a summer road-trip with your family, would you load up your car and your kids without a clear idea of how to reach your destination? Or, would you use tools (like an atlas or a map) carefully developed by experts who have already traveled the same path to navigate your way, thus making your trip more accurate and direct?

Just as the atlas assists the long distance road traveler, *Live Life! Be Young, Black and Successful* will help you, the success-seeking, young, African-American, navigate your road enabling you to more swiftly and accurately attain what you desire.

How Did They Do It?

Listening to successful young African-Americans publicly talk about their lives and their accomplishments sometimes gives the impression that they are subtly taunting "average" or "normal" brothers and sisters for not achieving what they have accomplished. Observers of these individuals may wonder whether or not these people are blatantly showcasing their accomplishments at the highest level of conceit. However, upon closer investigation, the reality is quite different. The truth of the matter is that these successful brothers and sisters have witnessed hundreds of people (all capable of creating the same levels of success) who were either not bold enough, not willing to sacrifice enough, or not persistent enough to reach their full potential. Take for example people you knew growing up who possessed the athletic, intellectual and/or artistic gifts to accomplish whatever they wanted but instead did little or nothing with their lives. Remember the naturally gifted singer at your school who everyone believed was going to be famous but never mustered the courage to sing in front of a crowd? What about the really smart kid at your school who everyone knew would go to college and eventually own his own business but ended up joining the neighborhood gang and was eventually sent to prison?

Knowing these facts about the millions of people who constantly ask, "How did you do it?" you probably can understand why successful young African-Americans do not have a lot of pity for those who have done less with their lives.

Are Successful Young African-Americans Naturally More Gifted?

Many people, particularly when it comes to sports, believe that natural ability predetermines who will and who will not be successful. For example, a person who is five feet tall is unlikely to have a career on a National Basketball Association (NBA) team, where most players are at least six feet tall.

While genetics has some impact on an individual's success, it definitely does not account for all. For example, if natural ability was the only factor in determining success in sports, how can you explain the outstanding accomplishments of 5-foot-5 1/2-inch Anthony "Spud" Webb, winner of the 1986 NBA Slam Dunk

Championship? And while contemplating the vastness of Webb's tremendous feat, also try explaining the accomplishments of Earvin "Magic" Johnson, who at 6-feet-9 inches became the tallest point guard in NBA history and a five-time NBA championship winner. Johnson's height and size categorize him more as a power forward or a center - not a point guard. Both Webb and Johnson achieved success in a professional league which assumed that you have to be tall to dunk and short to play point guard. So, do not believe the argument that individuals are "naturally" created for the success they achieve. Understand that through hard work, persistence and Faith all things are possible.

The Canvas: Creating the Mindset for Young, Black Success

Developing the Mindset to Be Young, Black and Successful

In your quest for success, one of the key components that you will have to master is gaining the mindset that will allow you to attain the type of prosperity that you seek. For years, professionally trained psychologists have dedicated their lives to studying human behavior and its relationship with success. In their quest for improved understanding of humans, some earth shattering theories have come from their research.

One theory of monumental importance was developed in the 1950's by psychologist Abraham Maslow. Maslow, often referred to as the father of Third Force Psychology – a theory based on the premise that all people are inherently good; that through a conscious evolution of attitudes, values, and beliefs, one becomes a self-actualized individual with the inner wisdom and confidence to guide their own life in a manner that is personally satisfying and socially constructive - proposed that all humans have certain needs that they work to fulfill during their lifetime. He believed that certain needs were more vital to the survival of humans than others, and thus ranked these needs in a specific order of importance. Furthermore, he believed that the successful fulfillment of these needs were critical to the healthy development of the adult human. For example, imagine a person who has been lost on a deserted island for 24 hours and has had nothing to eat or drink. If given a choice to drink a container of water or eat a package of food, which of the two do you think he would take first? Of course, he would drink the container of water. Why? Because a person can go without food for weeks, but can only last a few days without water. Satisfying the need of thirst is greater than satisfying the need of hunger. Maslow illustrated his concept of human needs and their order of importance in the form of a pyramid. The pyramid became widely known during the 1960's as Maslow's Hierarchy of Needs (see chart below).

In Maslow's hierarchy of needs, all humans start at the bottom of the pyramid - striving to fulfill their psycho-social or basic needs first before progressing further in their psychological development. Maslow defines our basic needs as being our need for water, food, oxygen, shelter, sleep, and sexual gratification. After meeting these basic needs, the individual continues up the hierarchy of needs seeking to satisfy his/her needs for safety, social belonging, self esteem, and the final need to actualize or express one's self – self actualization. Maslow believed that each of these "need" categories are essential to the healthy development of the human psyche. He also believed that each person is aware when one or more of these needs are lacking. In this book, we will not go into detail

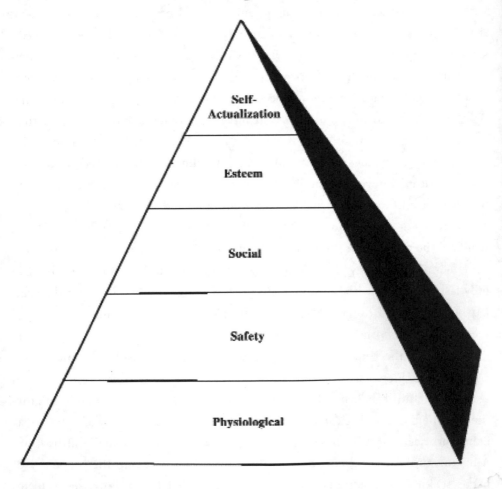

Maslow's
Hierarchy of Needs

Self-Actualization

Esteem

Social

Safety

Physiological

about all of Maslow's "need" categories. For our purposes, we will only discuss the greatest and best known of Maslow's hierarchy of needs and how it relates to young, Black success - self actualization.

Self-Actualization

"A musician must make music, an artist must paint, a poet must write, if he is to be ultimately at peace with himself. What a man can be, he must be. This need we may call self-actualization.... It refers to man's desire for self-fulfillment, namely to the tendency for him to become actually in what he is potentially: to become everything that one is capable of becoming...."

- Abraham Maslow

When analyzing significant accomplishments achieved by young African-Americans, you will find at the core of that achievement a man or woman who has actualized his/her "self." Great accomplishments cannot occur until the individual understands and actively works to fulfill his/her innate desire to reach his/her potential. Whether it be Michael Jordan's feat of winning five NBA championships; Tiger Woods' achievement of being the youngest player to win the career Grand Slam with wins at the Masters, U.S. Open, British Open and PGA Championship; or Venus and Serena Williams' wins at Wimbledon; on some level, these individuals had to realize their potential, discover the proper means to activate their ability, then create these realities in their lives.

The process of first understanding who you are and what you believe then making those things become a part of your "self" is a process that all successful people have gone through – and you must do the same if you are to achieve comparable success. If you are unsure what constitutes your "self", take time daily (through prayer or meditation) to concentrate and discover what you are about and what things are of utmost importance to you. Begin drawing a mental picture of the type of person you ultimately wish to become. Then slowly but surely, let your "self" emerge. Do not be hampered by other people's visions of what you ought to be. Develop the courage and the insight to decide the kind of lifestyle that will be of greatest benefit to you. Understand that this process takes time. For some, actualizing one's self takes weeks. For others, it occurs during the course of many years. In your process, here are some other tips offered by Terrance Malkinson in an article titled, *Self-Actualization and Your Career*, that will help you self-actualize:

1. Make all of your choices growth choices, with each decision moving you toward your potential.
2. Discover what you really want in life and set goals and objectives that will serve as milestones to achieve your vision of your future.
3. Listen to the impulsive voices that come from within rather than others' voices. Do not focus on how you are expected to feel or on the need to impress or be liked by others.
4. Identify your defenses and find the courage to give them up. Be a courageous risk-taker and dare to be unique. Be willing to risk unpopularity by disagreeing with others.
5. Assume responsibility and seek experiences that stretch your boundaries and move you toward higher levels of personal growth and development.
6. Experience each and every moment totally, living your life to the fullest. Do not feel threatened or frightened by the unknown.
7. Accept yourself and have a realistic perception of your reality. Look within yourself for the answers and take responsibility for yourself and your behavior.
8. Become skilled at interpersonal relations. Share empathy, kinship, intimacy, tolerance, respect, friendship and benevolence to others. Laugh at yourself and your imperfections but never make comments that hurt others.

Other Keys to Developing the Success Mindset

"Anything that can go wrong, will."
                              -Murphy's Law (Traditional version)

Another essential component in preparing your mindset for success is to adopt the mental approach used in Murphy's Law - anything that can go wrong, will go wrong. Originally stated by Edward A. Murphy, Jr., a rocket engineer for the United States Air Force, the phrase was coined after Murphy discovered all sixteen pieces of an experiment that he assigned someone to put together were installed incorrectly. Popular thought says only focus on the "best" things that can happen in the activity you are pursuing. However, while thinking about how things will go "right", be conscious of the possibility that things can go "wrong." Taking time to consider potential errors ensures that adequate preparation and attention is given to your endeavors.

Over the years, scientists and engineers have embraced the reasoning demonstrated in Murphy's Law to ensure greater degrees of success in their lines of work. Take for example industrial engineers who design parts and assist in the creation of instruction manuals that accompany these parts for products that require assembly after they are purchased (i.e. entertainment center, computer desks, book cases, etc.). These engineers make it a professional practice to develop parts and manuals with full knowledge that people are more likely to assemble the product incorrectly rather than correctly. So in their adherence to Murphy's Law, these engineers attempt to create parts and manuals that only allow the product to be assembled one correct way (i.e. designing parts with grooves that only slide in one way). Again, Murphy's Law automatically assumes that the part will be assembled incorrectly when given a choice. I have witnessed successful African-Americans use this mental approach countless times in their professional and personal lives. Each time I have observed people use Murphy's Law in their approach, the following two things have occurred:

First, whether it is for a business meeting, athletic team try-out or church committee, people who embraced this approach were better prepared and (consciously or unconsciously) took control of the events surrounding them. Why? Because people who are prepared, talk, move, and act more confidently than people who are less prepared. When people are certain they know what's going on, they develop an insatiable desire to share their knowledge with others. This desire creates confidence, and confidence is the cornerstone to success. Confidence is what successful people use to influence the thoughts and actions of others. Confident people are decision-makers, and you want to be the same.

Second, people who trained themselves to expect the worse were less likely to operate in what I term M.O.I.'s (moments of ill-preparedness). We have all experienced M.O.I.'s. M.O.I.'s occur in our lives due to our lack of preparation. For instance, many of us experienced our first M.O.I.'s in school. Remember the time when you sat down to take a test, then realized that you were not capable of answering the questions because you did not study? Remember those feelings of uncertainty that accompanied your lack of preparation? These are classic M.O.I.'s - moments when you were your least confident, least persuasive and least engaged. As you discover yourself embracing this mindset, you will notice that detailed preparation will ensure your success.

Optimize Your Opportunity

"A pessimist sees the difficulty in every opportunity; an optimist sees the opportunity in every difficulty."

\- Sir Winston Churchill

There are times when you will be full of great ideas for attaining success. During these times, your soul will supply you with hundreds of viable options to create the successful lifestyle you desire. Although you are capable of actualizing all of your great ideas, there is only one idea that is ideally suited for the particular situation you are in presently. This idea is called your optimal opportunity. Work to develop this opportunity first before starting other potential opportunities. The optimal opportunity is the one that naturally fits the time, financial resources and personal connections available to you at the present time. An example of a person who optimized his opportunity at a young age is Jermaine Dupri Mauldin (a.k.a. Jermaine Dupri or JD), President and CEO of So So Def Recordings. As a music industry writer, producer and company executive, JD learned that by focusing exclusively on his opportunity, he could produce the results he desired to achieve. As early as the age of three, JD began his involvement in the music industry. JD's father, a musician and former road manager, exposed Jermaine to the world of music by allowing him to attend studio sessions for R&B band, Brick. J.D.'s father toured with Brick as a drummer. JD was so thrilled by the sessions that he eagerly wanted to learn how to play the drums. He became so proficient playing drums that he knew the entire Brick drum track catalog by the age of five.

JD continued the optimization of his early opportunity by touring and performing as a breakdancer with a variety of well-known artists like Diana Ross, Herbie Hancock, Cameo, Whodini, Run-DMC, Grandmaster Flash and the Fat Boys - all before the age of thirteen. JD used these early experiences combined with his father's knowledge about the industry to discover and develop his first successful group - Kris Kross, who sold more than 8 million copies worldwide. Coincidentally, around the same time, JD saw a trio of young girls named Second Nature whom he believed also had tremendous potential.

However, he knew he would only be able to focus on one group at a time. Jermaine recalls, "I can't say that I was too young, but I didn't think I could work both of them and get them both record deals." As a result, he decided to let Second Nature go. They eventually got a deal with LaFace Records under the name TLC. Although some might feel that JD missed the opportunity to sign both Kris Kross and TLC, JD understood that by attempting to do so, he might not have been able to give each group the attention they deserved. The lesson to be learned from JD's story is to hone in and cultivate your optimal opportunity now. You will find by doing so that you will create optimal opportunities in the future for the other great ideas that you have.

Failing to Optimize Your Opportunity

"When you are not practicing, remember someone is practicing and when you meet him, he will win."

– Ed Macauley

Remember the group Arrested Development? You may recall that it was 1992 when Arrested Development blazed onto the music scene with their debut album, *3 Years, 5 Months and 2 Days in the Life of...* The album was a monumental success, selling four million copies worldwide. No one could deny the group's incredibly seductive and unique sound effectively titled Life Music. Songs like Tennessee and People Everyday captivated audiences in ways rarely seen.

Arrested Development continued their success well into 1993, playing at various concerts in cities throughout the country. The group received numerous awards including: two Grammy awards for Best New Artist and Best Rap Album; a Soul Train Music Award; an MTV Best Rap Video of the Year Award; and, a Rolling Stone Band of the Year Award. Arrested Development experienced so much success on their first project that Speech, co-founder and lead vocalist of the group, stated that the group would be around for another "ten to twelve years." So, if Speech and the rest of the group understood the opportunity they were sitting-on, why was *3 Years, 5 Months and 2 Days in the Life of...* the last successful project for Arrested Development? The answer is quite simple: Arrested Development failed to optimize their opportunity. After releasing *3 Years, 5 Months and 2 Days in the Life of...* and the *Unplugged* album (which was only a live version of the same songs), Arrested Development faded away for nearly two years until the release of their second album *Zingalamaduni* - a failure when compared to the record sells of their first project.

During the time between production of their first and second albums, inner conflicts clouded the group's efforts. Speech, rumored as being an overpowering and relentless control freak, was blamed for creating dissension within the group. His conduct led group singer, Dionne Farris (whose vocals contributed greatly to the success of the song, Tennessee), to leave the group for a solo career. After Farris' departure, Arrested Development officially announced their break-up. This announcement came only three years after Speech's prediction of long-lasting success.

If Arrested Development only had the wisdom and foresight to put aside their differences and optimize their opportunities, their success would not have been so short-lived. Don't allow yourself to be short-sighted. Create in your psyche how an opportunity will be optimized when it is presented.

Alan F. Daniels

Lots of Ideas, Lots of Energy, No Focus – Bad Combination

"The weakest living creature, by concentrating his powers on a single object, can accomplish good results while the strongest, by dispersing his effort over many chores, may fail to accomplish anything. Drops of water, by continually falling, hone their passage through the hardest of rocks but the hasty torrent rushes over it with hideous uproar and leaves no trace behind."

- Og Mandino

Do you have an excess of ideas on how to create success in your life? Do you have plenty of energy to make these ideas reality? However, do you try to implement too many of your ideas at once, subsequently, getting nothing of significance accomplished? If this is your problem, do not feel bad – you are not alone. From my studies of people who have fallen short of success, the fatal mixture of "lots of ideas, lots of energy and no direction" has caused numerous failures regardless of the task or objective. The trouble is not having thousands of thoughts and mounds of energy – most people with enormous levels of success have both. The problem occurs when you combine these attributes with no focus. Lack of focus generally leads to debilitating results such as confusion, loss of attention to details and frustration. In your search for excellence and success, guard yourself from falling prey to this deadly mix of actions. The key is to focus your efforts like Alan F. Daniels, thirty-two year old Founder, Chairman and CEO of RealEstate.com. During RealEstate.com's three-year existence, Alan was able to raise more than $60 million in venture capital to fuel the business. Alan discovered through his life experiences that focus and an overwhelming commitment to concentration were the primary tools that allowed him to escape the grasps of mediocrity, poverty and destructive means of life.

Born the first child of a single mother who was only fifteen years his elder in (Overtown) Miami, FL, Alan understood the meaning of hard times. Although he grew up in an environment that others might perceive as hopeless, Alan was fortunate – he was the son of a determined mother who never gave up and who always encouraged him to think for himself. Alan's mother graduated from high school the same year Alan was born. Alan grew up and received a number of academic and athletic scholarships upon his graduation. As Alan puts it, "I was able to understand and adapt to things at a young age, school was relatively easy for me – I never studied." In an effort to continue his education, Alan decided to attend Florida A&M University in Tallahassee, FL using his academic scholarships. During his first year in college, Alan signed up for an Algebra class as well as several other classes. Because school came easy to Alan, he aced all of his tests although he rarely attended class. On one faithful day, Alan's Algebra professor called Alan into her office to make him aware of the attendance policy that Alan had been violating all semester. As a result of the violation, the professor notified Alan that he was going to receive an "F" for the class. Alan was crushed - he had never failed a class before. In an effort to salvage his college career, Alan was able to get his teacher to compromise and give him an "I" (Incomplete) instead of an "F" for the course.

However, due to Alan's continued lack of focus and participation in his other classes, he eventually lost his scholarship the next semester. Dejected and confused, Alan left Florida A&M to enter basic training with the Army National Guard in search of the discipline he desperately needed. After returning from basic training – redirected and driven to succeed, Alan re-enrolled into Florida A&M and received an "A" in the course. The experience taught Alan a valuable lesson:

> I learned that it's not enough to have natural ability without focus and commitment. With that, I say to every young, Black person that has a dream, or goal, or vision is that anything that you want to do (if you believe is your God-given gift to the world), you can do it. You simply do it by focusing and by possessing a willingness to commit. Commitment is something that perseveres everything. I had to sell my sports car and condo to start my company. But, because I was committed and focused to a purpose (not something that could disappear into thin air) that I experienced something no one could take away from me. They can repossess your material possessions, but they can't repossess your commitment.

Discipline Your Mind to Produce the Results You Desire

"Concentration is my motto – first honesty, then industry, then concentration."
- Andrew Carnegie

Concentration is key to the attainment of your personal goals and objectives. To attain optimal concentration levels, rid your mind of all extraneous thoughts that will prevent you from giving your undivided attention to your desired objectives. Determine what are productive and non-productive expenditures of your time and energy, then devote yourself to all activities that you deem productive. In your quest for success, understand that life is a war divided into separate spiritual, emotional, physical, and financial battles. In order to fight these battles properly, you will have to armor yourself with a fitting ensemble of weapons to compete against these opposing forces.

For example, in your spiritual battle to find and/or become closer to God, know that you will have to fight sin and the variety of ways sin can enter and destroy your life. Sin often takes the form of drunkenness, drug-addiction, sodomy, fornication, over-indulgence, greed, stealing, and killing, to name a few. Sin attempts to hide the face of God and cause separation from Him. To prevail successfully in this battle, equip yourself with weapons like the Holy Scriptures, hearing and studying the word of God, and/or simply listening to God within yourself.

In your emotional battles to experience unconditional or "true" love with other people like friends, relatives, and significant others, know that you will have to fight the enemies of this camp which are hate, distrust, greed, envy, and low self-esteem. Use the weapons of self-love, self-respect, and self-trust to ward off these rivals. Two things happen when these tools of war are employed:

First, when you create love, respect, and trust for yourself, you allow yourself to freely and unconditionally be able to love, trust, and respect others. Second, through your manifestation of these qualities, you compel yourself to only allow others in your life who reciprocate love, respect, and trust for you – keeping those who attempt to hate, distrust, or envy you at bay.

To win the battle on the physical front, start by conquering your body - making it a castle-like fortress free from illness, ailments, and disease. Keep your body safe and secure by building a high wall around it constructed with the brick stones of healthy eating, safe-sexual practices, adequate rest, and regular exercise. For added security, surround your fortress and wall with a moat filled with sufficient levels of drinking water for proper hydration. And last, defeat the opponents attacking you on the financial front like interest rates, credit cards, taxes, rents, insurance payments, and utility bills by first understanding that the creators of these external forces (i.e. banks, utility and insurance companies, and various state and federal government agencies) are nothing more than the results of the combined wills and collective self interests of other people. Know that the successful completion of your goals and objectives will not always be aligned with these institutional devices. For that reason, prepare yourself to battle these wills with strategic financial planning like: detail-oriented organization of personal financial documents; proper budgeting and allocation of financial resources; and expert financial advice from financial planners. So, don't allow these obstacles to prevent you from accomplishing your goals and objectives. Use your concentration to become the victor in your battles and ultimately win your war.

The Law of Relationships

"If my life is better as a result of you being a part of it, then I can and will develop reasons to continue involving you in my life."

- Unknown Author

There are certain time-tested and proven natural laws that govern our lives - laws that have been around since the beginning of mankind. The successful adult human understands and abides by these natural laws to accomplish the goals he/she wants to achieve. Successful people understand that if they do not give proper attention to these laws, disharmony and tension will begin to manifest themselves in their lives. The key to success is to uncover these laws and to incorporate them into the daily aspects of your life. Some of the natural laws I am referring to are: the laws of conservation, the laws of return, the laws of balance, the laws of power and the laws of compensation and compromise, and the law of relationships. A detailed description of all of these natural laws is too extensive to be covered in this book alone. However, at the foundation of the law of relationships, there exists a fundamental belief that drives most human thought and action. This belief, known as the Natural Human Principle, states that "humans (despite their circumstances) naturally desire to do things they believe will make their lives better - not worse." This concept appears to be simple, but it's amazing how many people don't utilize it in their day-to-day attempts to understand and to influence human behavior. For example, American businesses routinely acknowledge the power of the Natural Human Principle by producing television and radio ads offering products that promise to help people lose weight, make more money, and improve their physical appearance. These businesses understand that they profit by persuading people to satisfy their need to do and be better. Conversely, The Natural Human Principle can also be used to understand the thought patterns of habitual drug users. In one of the most ironic ways imaginable, people abuse drugs in an attempt to make their lives better through escape. Although their actions ultimately do nothing but make their lives worse, the overriding belief is that the drug will make them feel better – at least temporarily. In both cases, The Natural Human Principle is the underlying reason driving the person's behavior. After fully understanding and adopting this principle, you will be on your way to learning and conquering a critical law of human nature – The Law of Relationships. The Law of Relationships states that: "If my life is better as a result of you being a part of it, then I can and will develop reasons to continue involving you in my life."

The Law of Relationships is an extension of people's desires to interact with other people that they believe will make their lives better. This Law helps you realize why people form relationships in their personal or business lives. For example, if you know someone who is reliable, trustworthy and assists you in times of need, you will find yourself creating reasons to continue your relationship with this person. Alternatively, if you know someone who is unreliable, distrustful and causes you emotional, spiritual or financial destruction, you will soon discover ways to remove this person from your life. In order to positively utilize the Law of Relationships, work on creating and developing resources, skills and abilities that people find valuable in life. For example, learn how to cook; become technologically adept; manage your finances effectively; resolve conflicts without confrontation; learn to listen; be independent; help others in times of need; and, respect people's space and property. There are others you can add to this list. Most dysfunctional relationships occur when people violate this Law. When people do not create value in the lives of others, healthy relationships are impossible to initiate and maintain. Therefore, the key to having successful business or personal relationships is to continually add value in the lives of people with whom you interact. By effectively using the Law of Relationships, you will ensure the development of healthy relationships of all kinds in the future.

Coming Out of "I" to Embrace "We"

"If your vision is not bigger than yourself, it is
without virtue and is doomed to fail."

- Unknown Author

Great men and women accept the fact that they have limits on their personal time, knowledge, abilities and resources. However, these rare human beings compensate their shortcomings by developing the unique ability to enlist the assistance of others to turn their ideas into reality. These individuals have discovered that they not only have to be able to convey the belief that their ideas will work -- they also have to convince people that their ideas will benefit the people who support them as well. In other words, they have to find a way to appeal to people's self-interest - the side of humans that asks the question "What's in it for me?" Robert Greene reinforces this statement in his book, *The Laws of Power*, by stating, "The quickest way to secure people's minds is by demonstrating, as simply as possible, how an action will benefit them." He goes on to state that, "Self-interest is the strongest motive of all: A great cause may capture minds, but once the first flush of excitement is over, interest will flag – unless there is something to be gained...The cause seduces but the self-interest secures the deal." Too often, I hear individuals in search of wealth and prosperity only think about how they will benefit from their proposed endeavors – always "me, me, me." Rarely, do these people consider how their actions will enrich the lives of others (particularly the people who they are seeking to influence). These self-centered individuals become so consumed by their own selfishness that the solutions to their desires always seem to escape their grasps. To fully understand and accept the mindset that will allow you to come out of "I" and embrace "we," let go of your primitive need to only satisfy yourself.

Understand that people (regardless of their sex, age, or gender) have goals and desires, too. Know that the closer you align yourself and your beliefs with the beliefs and needs of the people you seek to capture, the more successful you will become in gaining their loyalty and trust. Do not make the mistake that the world revolves around you and that people are obligated to give you their support. If you do so, be prepared to encounter what Greene calls "silent enemies" – resistors that you have created from your lack of acknowledging the thoughts and ideas of others. Avoid creating these types of enemies, for they can play a big part in preventing you from gaining needed support in actualizing your dreams.

LIVE LIFE!

Anything and Everything is Possible!!

"Go forth ye young man and dream. Dream hard, dream long, dream wise. Dream about whatever your mind leads you to dream. But, for God's sake – never stop dreaming."

- Unknown Author

Dreams are like streams where great ideas flow. And like streams, they often flow into areas that are boundless and never ending. Take advantage of your ability to dream. Spare no expenses: for there are none. To demonstrate the power of dreaming, imagine being the youngest African-American selected to pilot a National Aeronautics and Space Administration (NASA) space shuttle mission. As you sit inside the pressurized crew cabin of the $1.7 billion shuttle - - heart racing and blood pressure rising, you realize that your time has come…

(T-minus ten seconds and counting)

Since beginning NASA's Astronaut Candidate Program at the Johnson Space Center (near Houston, Texas), you have always dreamed of this moment. Even during your previous days as a jet pilot in the United States Air Force, you knew you wanted to be an astronaut and that one-day you wanted to travel to space. However, you weren't fully aware of the intense training activities that you would have to endure in order to fly this mission. First, there were the roughly one thousand hours of coursework required by NASA that you had to study and ascertain. Classes on shuttle systems, mathematics, geology, meteorology, guidance and navigation, oceanography, orbital dynamics, astronomy, physics, and materials processing were all part of the program...

(T-minus nine seconds and counting)

Next, there were the many hours of training specifically designed for pilots of a space shuttle mission. You spent forty hours training in the NASA T-38 aircraft fighters practicing the steep landing approaches experienced during a space shuttle return back to Earth. Soon afterward, you put in thirty more hours training in the altitude chamber where you were placed in a spacesuit then submerged in a big water tank known as the WET-F – in order to simulate the weightless environment experienced in space. You knew that preparing to be a pilot astronaut was going to be a daunting task, but never in your wildest dreams did you think it would be like this...

(T-minus eight seconds and counting)

Next, there were the simulators where you and your crew of astronauts learned how to fly the shuttle and practice every aspect of your mission. The shuttle had a great number of systems -- electrical, environmental, propulsive, guidance and navigation, and data processing to name a few -- that all had to be learned and mastered. In the beginning, you spent a considerable amount of time reading manuals and workbooks for each system. Then, you progressed to an interactive computer called the Regency trainer which allowed you as the pilot of the mission to bring up a screen blueprint of any system in the shuttle and turn switches on or off with the touch of a finger. The Regency trainer gave you the opportunity to "get your feet wet" preparing you for the true test of your piloting capabilities - the mission simulator...

(T-minus seven seconds and counting)

The mission simulator integrated all parts of the shuttle's systems into the same set of computers, so that the simulator operated the same way a shuttle would in flight. Since it is impossible to "test drive" a shuttle to space, the mission simulator was the only way that you and your crew were going to learn how to fly the shuttle. Each member of your crew spent eight to twelve hours a week working through various problems, glitches and malfunctions that could occur during an actual flight. The crew's performance in the simulator ultimately determined whether or not you were going to be granted permission to fly the mission. With a lot of hard work and a large degree of dedication and teamwork, your crew masters the mission simulator and is given their launch papers by NASA to fly...

LIVE LIFE!

(T-minus six seconds and counting)

So, you're back inside the cockpit preparing for launch. (Five…, Four…, Three…, Two…, One… Houston, we have lift off!) Suddenly, you start to feel the teetering of vibrations being caused by the two rocket-powered engines firing-up behind you. As the shuttle slowly powers up from the launch pad continuing on its dynamic journey to outer space (progressively passing through the mesosphere and the beginning layers of the ionosphere), you begin to feel the weight of gravity pressing against your chest making it difficult for you to breathe. After passing through the ionosphere and entering into outer space, you feel somewhat reassured knowing that the most violent part of your journey has passed. You decide at that moment to look out the cargo bay window and experience in all of its beauty and splendor your first glimpse of this place we call Earth. In one bold and picturesque view shot, you witness the summation of human thought and ingenuity throughout our millions of years of existence on this planet. It is at this breath-taking moment while considering all that it required to make this moment a reality, that it hits you -- anything and everything - with enough courage, hard work, determination and Faith - is possible.

All Eyes on Me

"I was in the store recently buying some fishing equipment and some people came up to me and said, 'Deion, we just praise the Lord for your testimony!' I didn't know anybody knew I was there. I wasn't thinking about my influence or who might be there while I was shopping. But these folks just came up and said thank you because they saw that I was having an influence because of my faith. You may never know who you've influenced in this world, but people are watching, and one way or another someone is being influenced by you."

- Deion Sanders, *Power, Money, & Sex:*
How Success Almost Ruined My Life

Do you sometimes feel like somebody's watching you? Well, in most cases you're right, someone is! Whether it is admiringly or resentfully, the culmination of who you are as a person is being assessed. So, in your dealings, adopt the mindset that all eyes are on you. Understand that other people's perceptions of you run deeper than just your physical appearance. There's more to it than that. Their perceptions take into account your overall outlook and your treatment of others. Know that every time you leave your house (whether you are taking a trip to the mailbox or a trip to your favorite restaurant) somebody has their eyes on you. It could be a cook – it could be a waiter – it could be a neighbor, but know that somebody, somewhere, every day is noticing what you're doing. So what does this have to do with success? The successful individual makes it a practice of behaving in such a manner that is consistent with the kind of person they want to be perceived as twenty-four hours a day, seven days a week. In addition, they treat all people that they encounter with respect. Why? Because they know the strength of their success is tied to their reputation - the perceived quality of their character. Never think that you are operating in isolation or in the dark. This world is much smaller than you might think. If you look closely at individuals of influence, you will discover that in addition to their acknowledged expertise, talents and abilities, possessing a favorable reputation ranks high on their list of attributes. This reputation allows these individuals to continue wielding the influence they possess. Without the good will of their reputations, the power and influence they hold would not exist.

Take for example Michael Jordan, former professional basketball player with the Chicago Bulls. In addition to being a six –time NBA championship winner, Michael was also a three-time gold medal recipient at the Olympic Games; selected as one of the 50 greatest players in NBA history; and rated number one on the Sporting News list of 100 Most Powerful People in Sports (1997). Michael's combination of several highly regarded American commodities: good looks, phenomenal athletic ability, and perhaps most importantly – a clean, scandal-free image -- greatly increased his marketing influence. Because of these attributes, advertisers were eager to court Michael for commercial endorsements of products.

As Michael's career, fame and squeaky-clean image continued, more endorsements came his way. He started with Nike and later signed contracts with McDonald's, Chevrolet, Coca-Cola, Gatorade and Wheaties cereal. His legendary basketball moves and ever-increasing fan base opened doors to business opportunities that had never been available to pro athletes before. Michael relished in the opportunities, attacking the business side as he did the basketball court with finesse, style, and a desire to be successful. This earned him countless dollars and world-renowned fame and even more fans. Michael's image was well received on and off the court, due in part to his strong sense of self, upbringing, and commitment to his family. In Michael's book, *For The Love Of The Game: My Story,* he describes his perspective on his growing influence and reputation:

> My life was changing and the way I was perceived was changing too. I was a father and a husband at home, but everywhere else I was Michael Jordan. And it seemed like everyone had an idea of what that meant except me. Early in my career, I really couldn't get a sense of who I was from the fan's perspective. I didn't feel as famous as people said I was. I was so focused on the game that I didn't have time to step back and consider my life in the context of everyone else. To some degree, I think that's why I was so well received. I wasn't acting. I wasn't trying to be something I wasn't. I always felt comfortable in the spotlight because I was just being myself. With my personality and the way I was raised, it would have been impossible to be something else. My parents never would have allowed me to get away with some kind of act.

Michael embodied the concept of all eyes on me – he lived it, he worked it and he capitalized on it. So, be like Mike and many other people of influence. Become conscious of the image you are projecting and the actions that you make. Both are critical to the development of your personal success. Do this and success will follow.

Maintaining Significant Increases

"... What I'm saying is if you have a formula that has produced significant increases in your life, stay with that formula. Don't try to deviate from a place that has produced favorable results. Always remember the old adage, 'if it ain't broke, don't fix it!' "

- Unknown Author

On April 23, 1985, a fiasco of tremendous magnitude in the history of American business was unveiled to the world. The Coca-Cola Company, head-quartered in Atlanta, Georgia, officially announced that it was discontinuing the old formula of Coke for a newer, more improved formula called "New Coke." According to company officials, this "new" Coke had been a winner in more than 200,000 blind taste tests and was cheaper to make than the old version. The Coca-Cola Company (already the leader in soft drink beverages) believed from its research that New Coke would take the company to new levels of success. After releasing New Coke, company executives were astonished to discover that millions of Americans decided that they hated New Coke before even tasting it and vehemently demanded the return of the old formula. Only three months after the initial announcement of New Coke (that's right three months!) and after millions of dollars were spent on marketing and advertising the new product, Coca-Cola announced that it was returning to the original Coke formula. In a final response to the tremendous public backlash of New Coke, Roberto Goizueta (then Chairman of Coca-Cola) stated publicly, "America, we have heard you."

What's the lesson to be learned from the New Coke disaster? Maintain significant increases in your life. Significant increases can be defined as the measurably improved benefits that have been directly created as a result of your success-oriented activities. Significant increases come in the forms of extra money, additional free time, increased peace of mind and more love. When you discover a method that significantly manifests bounty and beauty in your life, stay with that formula. Don't deviate from the source. Deviation often leads to disaster – and disaster is not desired. When you maintain significant increases, you will keep the prosperity you generate.

Let the Truth Be Told About the Dollar

"Money is important – it's terribly important. It's just as important as the food and clothes that it buys, the shelter that it affords, the education that it provides, and the bills that it pays. Money is important to anyone living in a civilized society, and to argue that it's not important is absurd. Let anyone who imagines that

LIVE LIFE!

he does not need money try to get along without it. Let us be realistic enough to face the facts of life, and demand from life the best that it can give. Nothing will take the place of money in the area in which money works."

- Dennis Kimbro, *Think and Grow Rich: A Black Choice*

"You will know the truth, and the truth will make you free."

- John 8:32

Since 1935 when Parker Brothers acquired the rights to the game from inventor Charles B. Darrow, Monopoly has become the leading proprietary game in the U.S. and throughout the Western world as well. Monopoly has been published in 25 countries worldwide and in 15 foreign languages and is the highest selling board game of all times. The practical lessons that are learned from playing the game have transcended all cultures, socio-economic levels, races and ages throughout its 60 years of existence. The game is symbolic of the capitalist values that Americans of all ethnicities have embraced and hold dear to their hearts. Monopoly reflects American desires to compete and conquer-to defeat and destroy. Its long lasting popularity is testament to the common principles it exudes. The more you know about the game Monopoly the more successful you are going to be in American society.

For those who are unfamiliar with Monopoly, the main objective is to become the wealthiest player through the buying, renting and selling of property. One of Monopoly's greatest attributes is its ability to give people, who might not have access to economic opportunities, an arena to compete where true equality is present. The game gives every player the same opportunity to win. For example, to start - each player receives the same amount of money from the Bank. Each player also starts with the same amount of property. In addition to starting with the same amount of money and property, all players have equal access to the rules of the game - preventing any one player from having an unfair advantage. Unlike the disparities often found in the American justice system, Monopoly provides fairness in jail sentencing, also. Players know beforehand all the ways that they could be sent to jail, the amount of time they will serve if sent, and the exact amount needed to secure bail. Monopoly eliminates all the inequities that young African-Americans have found or find present in American society - leaving only the individual player's business savvy and a small degree of chance as the determining factors for his/her success. Where else in "real life" do you find this kind of parity in economic opportunity?

As you play Monopoly, you soon discover that possessing large sums of Monopoly money and owning high-valued, Monopoly properties are the major keys to winning the game. You quickly realize that you have to work diligently to accumulate as many pieces of property available, build as many houses and/or hotels that you can afford on that property, and then charge other players' large sums of money when they land on your property. Otherwise, you may end up facing financial destruction in the deepest depths of poverty. It is definitely survival of the fittest; either eat or be eaten. The intensity created by Monopoly makes players forget they are playing a game. However, in order to discover the truth about the American dollar, go a step further and correlate the game of Monopoly with the financial game present in American society. For example, try to use Monopoly money in the real world to buy a new car at an automobile dealership. After the salespeople laugh at you and you are possibly arrested, you will find that Monopoly money holds no power in American society – only U.S. currency is accepted. Yet in Monopoly, Monopoly money, not U.S. dollars represents ultimate power. Try to purchase Monopoly property with money from another board game and you will be denied. Attempt to purchase Monopoly property with U.S. currency and you will discover that it too would not be accepted. Why? Because Monopoly players have mutually agreed to abide by the rules of the game which states that Monopoly money is the currency used for exchange. This collective belief in the game's rules is what makes Monopoly money more valuable than any other type of currency within the context of the game. Take away a player's belief in or conformity to the game's rules and you will discover that Monopoly money no longer holds its same level of power. Take away the collective belief and group conformity and you will have anarchy.

So, the truth is neither Monopoly money nor U.S. dollars by themselves have any value. An American dollar is no more than a piece of green-dyed cotton with a picture of a dead president on the front. Only when you combine these forms of currency with a collective belief does a "real" value exist. Just like the Monopoly players who collectively agree to use Monopoly money as their common currency, American citizens have collectively agreed to use the American dollar as our tool of commerce.

Another "Truth" Exposed

Another truth that needs to be told about the American dollar is that it is all but an infinite resource. The U.S. Treasury's Bureau of Engraving and Printing (BEP) produces approximately 37 million currency notes each day with a face value of about $696 million. Forty five percent of the notes printed are the $1 denomination. The paper that the BEP uses to produce American currency is composed of 75 percent cotton and 25 percent linen. So as long as the good mother Earth continues to produce the cotton that is used to make the dollar, there is potentially no end to the amount of currency that can be created.

The true problem that occurs presently and has occurred historically is in how the dollar has been circulated – only 1% of the nation possesses 99% of the wealth. As long as people collectively believe/buy into the American dollar's perceived value, true power will belong to the people/institutions that print it, regulate it, enforce conformity to it and/or decide how it will be used or distributed.

What does all this mean to young African-Americans attempting to find success in American society? It means that African-Americans of all ages have to continue to fight for inclusion and representation in institutions that print, regulate, enforce and distribute American currency (i.e. investment and community banks, government institutions like the Department of Treasury and the Federal Reserve, the Securities and Exchange Commission and various money-delivering functions in major U.S. corporations). By doing so, young, success-oriented African Americans will create access to opportunities previously unavailable to generations of African-Americans in the past.

QUINCY BENTON

The Easel: Supporting the Canvas of Young, Black Success

Angels on Earth

Good mentors are important to the well-rounded and long-lasting development of the success-seeker. True success will not be found where good mentoring does not exist. Although the concept of mentoring has been around since the beginning of man's existence, the word mentor itself has its first known origins in an epic poem titled, The Odyssey, written over 2500 years ago by the Greek poet Homer. The Odyssey greatly influenced much of Greek literature during this period. The poem's human and supernatural characters and gods were heroes worshipped in many parts of Greece and eventually became known worldwide. Characters like Zeus (Supreme God and King of Olympus), Athena (Goddess of Wisdom and Daughter of Zeus), Poseidon (God of the Sea and Earthquakes) and Odysseus (King of Ithaca) had a tremendous impact on Greek society. Even today, high school students in Greece as well as in America are exposed to The Odyssey by the time they graduate.

The story of The Odyssey begins ten years after the Trojan War. The main character, Odysseus, and his troops have yet to return from the war and are thought to be dead. All the other kings and chieftains who battled in the war have safely arrived in their native lands or died, but nobody in Ithaca has heard from Odysseus. Although he is considered dead by most people in Ithaca, Odysseus is still alive; however, his troops have perished. Odysseus desperately wants to return home, but Poseidon (God of the Sea and Earthquakes) has a personal vendetta against Odysseus for blinding his son Polyphemus (the oneeyed Cyclops). Since the only way that Odysseus can return home is by sea, Poseidon creates numerous obstacles to prevent Odysseus from getting back to Ithaca.

During the ten years that Odysseus has been away, the noblemen of Ithaca and the surrounding states have converged upon his palace hoping to win the hand of his wife, Penelope.[1] Penelope refuses to remarry; but knows that if Odysseus does not return that she will someday be forced to do so. While the suitors stay at the palace trying to change her mind, they waste the wealth of Odysseus' estate for their own pleasure and corrupt many of his servants. Odysseus' son, Telemachus, witnesses first hand all of the corruption that has taken place in his father's and mother's palace but lacks the courage or wisdom to

---

1 Ithaca is a matriarchal society, so Odysseus is king because he is married to Penelope, the hereditary queen.

take action. Taking the form of Mentor, a loyal and trusting friend of Odysseus, Athena motivates and encourages Telemachus to go find his father and reclaim their kingdom.[2] Athena also provides Telemachus with needed guidance, as Mentor, throughout Telemachus' journey. Telemachus does not find his father, but the trip dramatically matures him and consequently becomes an important step in preparing him to one day succeed his father as king.

The spirit of the Creator speaks to us in a similar fashion utilizing individuals like Mentor to guide us through our personal trials and tribulations. It is during these times that we receive spiritual and emotional guidance from the Creator to handle the difficulties we are faced. These mentors are the Creator's "Angels on Earth." Listen carefully and intently when these individuals appear in your life. Know and trust in the belief that the appearance of these mentors is part of the Creator's divine plan of intervening into your life for the ultimate good of your existence. Understand that once you have obtained the necessary knowledge and wisdom needed from these individuals, you will be charged with the responsibility to act as a good mentor to others.

A word of caution about mentors

Make sure that the individuals whom you choose as mentors are mentoring you in areas in which they are knowledgeable. Understand that good mentors have flaws. For example, would you want someone who has a successful landscaping business, but has been married five times to give you advice about how to start and maintain a productive and loving marriage? Hardly. However, it probably would be beneficial to receive guidance from this person regarding the business of landscaping. In your search for competent mentors, ask yourself the following: Does this person possess the lifestyle that I truly desire? What are the pros and cons of this person's way of life? Are the cons ones I can live with?

Ask yourself these questions openly and honestly to determine if this is the

2 In Greek mythology, gods and goddesses have very special relationships with their human subjects. Although they are supernatural and omniscience beings, they show favoritism and did like to their human subordinates. The Goddess Athena strongly favors Odysseus and his son Telemachus. Additional note: Greek gods and goddesses also possess the ability to intervene in human lives by appearing as other people, animals or objects; thus, explaining Athena's appearance as Mentor.

type of individual from whom you should receive counseling. If you decide that this person meets your criteria, work diligently to solidify your relationship. You will discover that your mentor will serve as a success-making tool all the days of your life.

Ayinde Jean-Baptiste

The Importance of Family

"When you stop making excuses, when you start standing with our mothers, when you stick it out with your family, when you start mentoring our young, when you

start teaching us to be humane, then we can build a new nation of strong people. Then your children will not join gangs, because they belong to a community."

- Ayinde Jean-Baptiste,
12-year-old speaker at the 1995 Million Man March

The most important factor in attaining success as a young, African-American is the possession of a loving and supportive family unit. Long-term success is difficult to achieve without the presence of a strong family dedicated to the lasting preservation of the family members. One successful young, African-American who has witnessed firsthand the importance of a supportive family unit is Ayinde Jean-Baptiste. When he was only 12, Ayinde was a featured speaker at the 1995 Million Man March on Washington. His speech at the March provoked international debate about the critical roles played by African-American men as well as showcased the passionate and articulate oratorical skills possessed by this gifted young man. When analyzing the tremendous impact that family has had in Ayinde's life, it becomes apparent that Ayinde's parents sowed the seeds of success early - starting with the careful selection of his name, Ayinde Shomari Couvil. Ayinde, which is Yoruba (a language spoken by people in Western Africa), means "we gave praises and he came." Shomari, which is Swahili (a Bantu language spoken on the East Coast of Africa), means "forceful." And, Couvil was given to Ayinde in honor of his paternal grandfather, Couvil Lauture.

In addition to putting careful thought in the selection of Ayinde's name, Ayinde's parents also put him in the proper environment to ensure his on going success. Exercising a bold option typically unused by most parents, Ayinde's parents decided to enroll him into Westside Preparatory School (on the westside of Chicago) at the tender age of 3 years old – a full two years before the starting age of most children entering kindergarten. After meeting with the principal of Westside (who coincidentally happened to be world-renowned educator Marva Collins), Ayinde's parent and Marva Collins both agreed that Ayinde was ready.

While at Westside, Ayinde and his fellow classmates were required to complete an arduous curriculum emphasizing the areas of language arts and math. In addition, students were required every morning to recite a school creed before starting each day.

After completing third grade, Ayinde left Westside and attended school at the Thomas Edison Regional Gifted Center. School officials at Thomas Edison were not as accepting of Ayinde's special circumstances and consequently required him to repeat third grade. However, after Ayinde finished the first quarter of third grade at Edison, Ayinde's teachers discovered that he was considerably ahead of his classmates academically and immediately moved him to the fourth grade. Ayinde continued his blistering pace through middle school and high school - graduating at the age of 16 from The Roycemore School in Evanston, Illinois. During his school years, Ayinde established an impressive academic record that included scoring a 1490 on the SAT, graduating in the Top 10% of his class with a 3.87 cumulative GPA and receiving a nearly full-tuition scholarship at Harvard University. For those fortunate enough to have a strong family support system like Ayinde's, you have no excuse and are required to achieve success. For those who do not have this type of support system, success is still attainable; however, may be more challenging to accomplish. This family unit does not have to consist of only members who are blood related. The family unit I am speaking about consists of individuals who are devoutly committed and completely focused on contributing actions that create success for each family member.

Good Timing

"To everything there is a season. A time for every purpose under heaven; A time to be born, And a time to die; A time to plant, And a time to pluck what is planted; A time to kill, And a time to heal; A time to break down, And a time to build up; A time to weep, And a time to laugh; A time to mourn, And a time to dance; A time to cast away stones, And a time to gather stones; A time to embrace, And a time to refrain from embracing; A time to gain, And a time to lose; A time to keep, And a time to throw away; A time to tear, And a time to sew; A time to keep silence, And a time to speak; A time to love; And a time to hate; A time of war, And a time of peace."

\- Ecclesiastes 3:1-8

Timing is always important to a comedian. If a comedian has good timing, his/her delivery flows smoothly and the critical role that timing plays often goes unnoticed. However, if a comic's timing is bad, the crucial part that timing plays in comedic success becomes apparent. Just as good timing is important to the aspiring comedian, so too is it important to the success-seeker. Similar to the life of a comedian where having good timing plays dual roles – having good timing on-stage (delivering well-thought and rehearsed jokes) and having good timing off-stage (being in "the right place at the right time" in order to get discovered), the life of the success-seeker contains identical timing elements. True success only appears in the life of the success-seeker after combining these two essential ingredients of good timing.

In my studies of people's beliefs about success, I have discovered that the duality that exists in having good timing is widely misunderstood. Contrary to popular belief, a comedian's effective telling of a joke or an individual's outstanding life achievement doesn't just happen because of some natural, unrefined, God-given ability. The comedian develops polished and well cadenced delivery and the success-seeker achieves noteworthy personal accomplishments from consistent and continuous practice.

However, neither the comedian nor the success-seeker (regardless of the level or intensity of practice) can fully attain success without being presented the right opportunity at the right moment in time.

Take Chris Rock for example. After dropping out of school at age 17 and working a variety of fast food jobs, Chris decided to follow his dreams and pursue a career in comedy. He began his pursuit by auditioning relentlessly at nightclubs throughout New York City to secure his first professional gig. Two years later, he debuted at *The Comic Strip*. Although he was allowed to perform at the club, Chris only received $6.00 a night for his efforts and had to stack chairs at the end of each performance. Despite his deplorable working conditions, Chris never gave up and never stopped practicing. Chris' father taught him at a very young age to work hard, be responsible, and be on time.

One day on his way to work, Chris noticed a fleet of luxury automobiles parked outside of the club. Curious, Chris asked around to discover what was going on. Unbeknownst to Chris, Eddie Murphy was in attendance and was coincidentally looking for new talent. Although Chris was not scheduled to perform, he begged the club manager to let him go on stage next. Confident and well-prepared, Chris gave an exceptional performance. In his words, Chris stated, "I killed! I probably haven't done that well (on stage) since."

Impressed with Chris' talents and skills, Eddie Murphy began recruiting Chris for various projects and eventually helped him land roles in two movies, *Boomerang* and *Beverly Hills Cop II*. The rest is history. Chris Rock has gone on to become a giant in the entertainment industry – starring in numerous television commercials and award-winning comedy specials as well as producing and hosting his self-titled, HBO comedy special, *The Chris Rock Show*.

So, in your quest for success, remember to prepare yourself fully for the opportunities you want to receive. Keep hopeful and prayerful that your opportunities will come. And when they do, be prepared for the powerful and wonderful things that will occur as a result.

Ananda Lewis

Is Knowledge Power??

"The individual who can do something that the world wants done will, in the end, make his way regardless of his race."

\- Booker T. Washington

Have you ever heard the saying, "Knowledge is power!" Do you believe the statement is true? Many people I have encountered have accepted this statement at "face value" without taking time to consider its validity. At some point, we all have witnessed people who have utilized their levels of knowledge and expertise to create powerful and meaningful lives. You only have to casually glance around to find people like neurologists, private consultants, mechanics and morticians who have created power from their knowledge. We know that the saying has some truth. However, if you are like most people, you have also noticed that everybody knows something. Ironically, most people know quite a bit about a variety of different things. So, if knowledge is power and everybody knows something, why aren't all people powerful? The answer can only be found once you dispel the myth that knowledge is power. Contrary to popular belief, knowledge is not power.

Knowledge only has the potential to create power. It is only when knowledge consists of self-empowering information, properly used and applied, that it becomes powerful. People who create power from their knowledge understand how to use knowledge for maximum return. People who just know a lot have information primarily consisting of nonsense – knowledge that does little to empower them as people.   Knowledge about the dates and times of a watched television show or knowledge about other people's personal business consumes and clogs their minds preventing self-empowering thoughts from entering and taking root. Consequently, this abundance of non-empowering information does little to assist these individuals in creating powerful and meaningful lives.

If your objective is to create power from the knowledge you possess, first rid yourself of non-empowering information. Do not make it a practice of harboring or searching for further nonsense. Second, fill your mind with empowering information like making stronger and more loving personal relationships, communicating more effectively or developing better techniques for healthy eating and living. Third, make sure you combine your empowering thoughts with action. Knowledge is only powerful when it is put to use. And last, heed the words of Ananda Lewis, when she states:

> Whatever you choose to do, learn every aspect of it. Don't go in blind. Don't go
> in letting someone know more about what you're supposed to do than you. If
> you want to be an actress, learn how to be a writer and a director. If you want

to be a cameraman, learn how to be an actor and a director. If you want to be a writer, learn how to be an editor and a copyrighter. So, you learn everything that surrounds your field. This gives you more expertise - the power to effectively communicate and to know what's going on. Expertise is something that you never lose. It will always to be with you. And, you'll always have a job in your field. If you can, play different positions. You will always stay on the team.

Counting Blessings

"Very few people are either satisfied with the way they look or with what they have, no matter how much it is. There seems no way ever to get enough of anything. Everybody is expected to be trying for a promotion, a better job, more money, more expensive clothing, a bigger house, to expand the business. Being content is out of the question, and we have the stress indicators to prove it. I'm trying to learn to relax and to be grateful for what I have."

- Janet Cheatham Bell, Author of
Victory of the Spirit:
Meditations on Black Quotations

In 1996, I was the owner of a private, in-home tutoring business in the Atlanta metropolitan area. Although the business only employed about ten part time tutors and was scarcely profitable, it paid huge returns in several ways. Not only did the tutors and I receive personal satisfaction by helping children improve academically, but we also developed close relationships with all of the families who were clients.

One particular client, a single African-American mother with a seven year-old daughter, made a lasting impression on me that I will never forget. I remember being initially impressed with this woman, because she seemed to possess everything that a person would need in life: a good paying, corporate job in the international flight division of a major airline, a spacious home and a luxury car. Since she worked at the airline, she had the added benefit of traveling internationally at no cost. Although her daughter was only seven, she could tell you vivid stories about their trips to Paris, the Philippines and

Egypt. In addition to private tutoring, her child also received private ballet lessons and private piano lessons. They seemed to have it all.

In order to get to her house, I had to drive by the estate of heavyweight boxing champion Evander Holyfield. At the time, Evander was in the process of putting the final touches on a new 52,000-square-foot home he was building on his property.

One evening, the mother and I happened to get into a discussion about this new home Evander was building. During the conversation, she commented, "I hope Evander's children know how truly blessed they are." Her comment shocked me because it was expressed with an unsaid but clearly implied meaning that Evander's children were "more" blessed than other children simply because their father had the ability to purchase a 52,000-square-foot home. Furthermore, she went on to state, "It must be nice to be able to buy such a beautiful house. His wife is so lucky!" All of this coming from a woman who seemed to have it all. I was shocked!

From our conversation, I was able to discover that the woman did not know Evander Holyfield or the members of his family personally. All of the assumptions she made about the Holyfield family were just that – assumptions. Why is this story important? It is significant because it shows some of our beliefs about blessings. For instance, how do we know if Evander Holyfield's children are "truly" blessed? This woman only had a superficial knowledge of the Holyfield family. She had no idea what went on inside the walls of Evander's house.

As I discovered that this woman's assumptions about Evander Holyfield's lifestyle were formed primarily from her outside view of Evander's holdings (the size of his home and property, etc.), I realized that I too had fallen into this trap. From my few encounters with this woman and her daughter - seeing their house and their car - I assumed they probably "had it all."

It is easy to assume an individual "has it made" by just looking at their accumulated worldly possessions. So, stop looking at other people's "blessings" and begin counting your own. Because realistically, the only blessings that we can legitimately count and accurately measure are the blessings that have been given to us by the Creator above.

How Do You Count Blessings?

First, start by understanding the meaning of a blessing. A blessing is the "unlimited goodness that only God has the power to know about or give to us." Blessings are exhibited in many ways in our everyday living.

Second, give thanks for the essential things you and your family have been given that are often overlooked. For example, be thankful for the food you have been "blessed" with to feed yourself and your family and for your personal good health and the health of friends and family around you. These probably sound like pretty common life ingredients that everyone should be thankful for, but I often come into contact with people who routinely complain about their circumstances, while taking for granted the many blessings they have.

I received an email that serves as a constant reminder of how blessed most of us are. The email read:

If you woke up this morning with more health than illness, you are more blessed than the million who will not survive the week.

If you have never experienced the danger of battle, the loneliness of imprisonment, the agony of torture or the pangs of starvation, you are ahead of 500 million people around the world.

If you attend a church meeting without fear of harassment, arrest, torture, or death, you are more blessed than almost three billion people in the world.

If you have food in your refrigerator, clothes on your back, a roof over your head and a place to sleep, you are richer than 75% of this world.

If you have money in the bank, in your wallet, and spare change in a dish someplace, you are among the top 8% of the world's wealthy.

If your parents are still married and alive, you are very rare, even in the United States. If you hold your head with a smile on your face and are truly thankful, you are blessed because the majority can, but most do not.

If you can hold someone's hand, hug them or even touch them on the shoulder, you are blessed because you can offer God's healing touch.

If you prayed yesterday and today, you are in the minority because you believe in God's willingness to hear and answer prayer.

If you can read this message, you are more blessed than over two billion people in the world that cannot read anything at all.

Considering this, you should begin to count other blessings in your life that are unseen, yet exist. These intangible blessings manifest themselves through the trust you are experiencing in relationships with your family, your spouse and your friends. Remember to be thankful for individuals that you love and trust who are experiencing healthy relationships in their lives, also. As God's children, always remember that He wants to bless us just as much as we want to be blessed. So, when asking for understanding from the Creator for areas in your life that you want to develop, remember to give thanks for the areas where you have experienced improvements. In order to keep the blessings flowing, create a daily ritual of reciting *The Jabez Prayer*:

> And Jabez called on the God of Israel saying, 'Oh, that You would bless me indeed, and enlarge my territory, that Your hand would be with me, and that You would keep me from evil, that I may not cause pain!' So God granted him what he requested.
>
> 1 CHRONICLES 4:10 (NKJV)

Using this simple prayer, you will soon be able to testify to the many miracles that will appear in your life.

The Tools: Painting the Picture of Young, Black Success

QUINCY BENTON

You Are What You Do!

"Excellence is an art won by training and habituation. We do not act rightly because we have virtue or excellence, but we rather have those because we have acted rightly. We are what we repeatedly do. Excellence, then, is not an act but a habit."

- Aristotle

Remember the famous saying, "You are what you eat!" Success works the same way: You are what you do! Restated in a different way: You are what you do regularly and consistently. This concept is extremely important to grasp if you are going to make a sincere claim to achieve whatever you want. For example, if you write on a regular basis, you are a writer. If you read on a regular basis, you are a reader. If you act on a regular basis, you are an actor.

The same is also true if you complain, procrastinate, or wish on a regular basis. In my observation of human behavior, I have noticed that people make claims to be many of the things they do not regularly and consistently practice, leaving ample room for non-achievement. We all know people who claim to be singers, musicians, comedians, entertainers, painters and so on whom we have never witnessed doing what they claim to regularly and consistently do. Maybe, you are even guilty of making claims but never making a consistent attempt to practice what you preach.

I often hear low or non-achievers use the excuse, "They wouldn't pay me, so I didn't do it!" But when we closely analyze the careers of successful, young African-Americans, we discover that these individuals possess skills that they were paid little or no money to develop, yet returned huge rewards as a result.

As a two-time Grammy award winner, six-time platinum recording artist and acclaimed TV sitcom and movie actor, James Todd Smith, better known to his fans and admirers as LLCoolJ, found-out that doing what he loved to do (regardless of whether he was paid to do it) paid-off handsomely in the long run. Growing up in the gang-infested streets of Queens, New York, life was not easy for this young man. At an early age, he witnessed his father brutally shoot his mother and grandfather with a 12-gauge shotgun. To make matters worse, his mother's boyfriend, a habitual cocaine user, physically and mentally abused him for four agonizing years of his life. Fortunate for LL, his mother and grandfather survived the shooting and his mother eventually left her boyfriend. Although these tragic incidents occurred, LL did not let them prevent him from succeeding in life.

At the age of 13, LL saw that hip-hop was growing in New York and he wanted to become a part of it. Rap artists like Kurtis Blow, Grandmaster Flash and the Furious Five and the Sugar Hill Gang were on the rise. Although he had little money, LL had big dreams of becoming a successful rapper. In his recent national best selling autobiography, *I Make My Own Rules*, he describes how a neighborhood friend and DJ at the time, Jay Philpot, first introduced him to the world of hip-hop. "He (Jay) would come over and ask my mother or my grandmother permission to take me to a party to work with him. We might make $50, but I would do it for free, for the attention. I did it for the love of the music, the love of holding the mike and rapping..." He goes on to state, "I was really feeling this thing called hip-hop. I wanted to perform all the time. I would hang out in joints like the Brown Door, an underground club in Queens, and listen to what was hot and try to get down. I would be at house parties, basements, anywhere I could rhyme and just hold the mike."

He would soon discover that his ability to continually practice his art and his dedication to succeed as a rapper would eventually pay-off; and pay-off big. LLCoolJ continues to be one of the most widely known and respected rapper/entertainers in the business.

So remember, you are what you do! If you don't do or practice success-oriented activities on a consistent and regular basis, guess what? You will never become what you claim to be. You're not an actor if you don't act! You're not a preacher if you don't preach! You're not an entrepreneur if you don't start businesses! The ability to continually practice success-oriented activities begins to separate those individuals who only talk about their dreams from those who make their dreams reality. I call it separating the takers from the taken, the shakers from the shaken, and the leaders from the led.

Raising the Standard

"No student ever attains very eminent success by simply doing what is required of him: it is the amount and excellence of what is over and above the required that determines the greatness of ultimate distinction."

- Charles Kendall Adams

Although I did not fully understand it at the time, I had the good fortune of having Mrs. Christine King-Farris, sister of the late Dr. Martin Luther King, Jr., as one of my professors at Morehouse College. Just imagine having direct access to the thoughts and insights of the sister to one of the greatest Americans in history.

The first major assignment that our class was given was a research project. Being the meticulous professor that she was, Mrs. Farris outlined each component of the project step-by-step in a detailed instruction packet. At the time, I was in my third year of college and was particularly focused on excelling academically in school. My goal for that year was to make all A's in my classes, so I was dedicated to putting my all into this project. I completed every step of the project exactly as Mrs. Farris had outlined in the instruction packet. I double-checked my paper several times, dotting every "i" and crossing every "t" before turning it in to make sure that I complied with all of her requests. I felt confident that I was going to receive an "A" on the project.

Three days later, I received my project back from Mrs. Farris. But, instead of the "A" that I had anticipated, there was a "C" marked on my project. I was devastated! I thought I had fulfilled all the requirements of the project. Confused, I went to Mrs. Farris to find out why I received a "C" on my project. Gazing into my eyes like a caring and concerned mother, she told me something that I have never forgotten. She said, "Son, in life, people who only do what is expected of them are average people. Average people go through life only doing enough to get by receiving "C's" in life. But, people who go above and beyond what is expected of them - and the expectations they have for their own lives - are above average people. Above average people are the ones who receive "A's" and "B's" in life." My life has not been the same since.

Are you one of those people who only does what is required, but expects above average results? Even worse, are you one of those people who does not meet the minimum requirements that you know you are capable of achieving, and as a result, categorize yourself as below average? Just like the grade "C", people who are average fall in the middle of the grading scale of life. Average people make little or no difference in the lives and hearts of others. Only those high-achieving men and women who consciously and consistently push themselves to higher levels of achievement make lasting differences in their lives and the lives of other people.

Step "Out-of-the-Box"

"An artist must be free to choose what he does, certainly, but he must also never be afraid to do what he might choose."

– Langston Hughes

Step out-of-the-box! Take time to think about how your approach can be different rather than the same. While searching for your unique approach, take into consideration successful strategies used by other people to produce the results you desire. However, don't let your search stop there. Attempt to discover how you can build on these successful strategies to create something new and original of your own. Begin to think of your thoughts as buried treasures; divine fortunes waiting to be excavated to better our community and our world. Like raw molten glass waiting to be heated, shaped and crafted to create exquisite pieces of sculpted glass, original thoughts or beliefs manifest themselves into similar forms of beauty in the real world. An innovative young African-American who has demonstrated the power of this ever important principle by carving out a career in an industry typically not pursued by young African-Americans - Kevin Jeffrey Clash, puppeteer and voice of Sesame Street's Elmo, has exemplified the power gained from stepping "out-of-the-box."

Born the third of four children in a household headed by two parents in (Turner Station) Baltimore, Maryland, life for Kevin was far from being ordinary growing

Kevin J. Clash

up. Although he was born into a creative family headed by creative parents, Kevin experienced a large part of his childhood being the "odd ball out." His brother was a phenomenal basketball player. His older sister was an intellectual. And his younger sister was into fashion. To make life more complicated, most of the kids in Kevin's neighborhood were only interested in playing sports or starting bands. When Kevin (at the age of ten years old) became so intrigued by puppets from watching shows like Sesame Street, he took it upon himself to pursue the art of building and performing puppets. This is where Kevin's journey began down the road of opposition faced by those who dare to step out of the box. Fortunate for Kevin, he had supportive parents that always backed him up:

My mother always took me to hobby shops so I could buy materials to build my puppets. She also taught me how to use her sewing machine, so I could make my puppets. My father contributed by helping me build a puppet stage and by driving me to various venues in the Baltimore area.

Kevin goes on to state:

When you've got parents who support you 100% and don't make you feel like you're doing something wrong, that's all you need. I don't care if it's one or two parents. It's about backing your child up 100% as far as what they want to do.

The support Kevin's parents gave him was important. But, it would have to contend with the pressures that Kevin would encounter from his peers in middle school and high school if he were to ultimately succeed.

During Kevin's middle school years, he began to share his fascination with puppets by bringing them to school and incorporating them into his school projects. "Since it (puppeteering) was so different – it wasn't sports, it wasn't music – people looked at me like I was crazy. People were saying, 'You sleep with your puppets… You do this with your puppets.' And, it wasn't until I started doing variety shows and doing television that people began to somewhat accept and appreciate what I was doing. But, still they would see it as a nerd type of thing. So, it wasn't until high school that things began to turn around for Kevin.

In high school, Kevin met a good friend named Tony Bartee. During the time that Kevin met Tony, he was starting this new technique of building puppet versions of his friends. Tony was one. His puppet was called Bartee. And there was another guy nicknamed Skylo who was the other. Skylo was real popular. All the girls at school loved Skylo. He was short and kind of a bully type. None of Kevin's puppets would look like his friends. They would just have his friend's names and the qualities of their personality.

Using his Bartee puppet, Kevin was able to become master of ceremonies for a variety show being held at his high school. Kevin describes the variety show as his domain. And through that domain, he was able to get back at students who heckled him when he didn't have the puppet on. Bartee became real popular after that.

On that day, Kevin's high school principal's secretary saw the show and just so happened to have a friend who worked at a major newspaper in Baltimore. The reporter was interested in meeting Kevin, so he came to Kevin's house. At the time, he had about twelve puppets that he had already built. After the reporter's meeting with Kevin, he was so intrigued that he interviewed Kevin and included Kevin's picture in a supplement of the paper called *Young World*. The article got around town fast. And because of that article, Kevin was asked to do shows locally around the Baltimore area. As a result of his performances, a local television station weatherman named Stu Kerr saw Kevin and was amazed. Stu had recently started a children's show at the station called *Professor Cool's Fun School*, but wanted Kevin to come in and audition for a new show that he was going to start called *Caboose*. Kevin took Bartee in to audition for Stu. Stu loved Bartee.

Kevin and Stu immediately hit it off. *Caboose* became Kevin's first professional puppeteering gig. And Stu became his first mentor. Kevin was still a senior in high school around this time. And was making about $200 a week doing *Caboose* with Stu. He was also an actor in the television union and doing two or three different shows at $25 a show during the weekend. Since Kevin was a child, he had always dreamed of working for Sesame Street after graduating from high school. After several unsuccessful attempts to work for Sesame Street, Kevin went on to work with the *Captain Kangaroo Show* after graduating from high school that year. While working on Captain, Kevin also began working as a puppeteer and an associate producer with a children's show called the *Great Space Coaster*. It was right around that time that Jane Henson (Jim Henson's wife) asked Kevin to come and work for Sesame Street. Kevin agreed and started working with Sesame Street when he was 19 years old. One day while working on the set of Sesame Street, Richard Hunt - a principal puppeteer with the Jim Henson company - came into the Muppet Room, the place where all the puppeteers congregated, and threw his puppet at Kevin. Because of the contempt that he had for the puppet, Richard asked Kevin to come up with a new voice for the doll. So, Kevin did what Richard asked and came up with a new, falsetto-pitched voice for the character. After hearing the voice, Richard agreed and decided that they should go to the producer of the show to get her approval for the new voice. The producer listened and agreed. And that is how Kevin started doing Elmo.

At that point, Kevin thought to himself, "If Richard couldn't make this puppet work, how am I going to make it work?" So, he decided to go to his mom's daycare center to observe children at the center. After interacting with the children, Kevin picked up some things that gave him an idea of what he wanted to do with the character. Soon after his visit, the writers and directors began to like what he was doing with Elmo. They liked it so much that they started writing more for the character.

After the season was over, Sesame Street's research department went out to find out which characters were working. They found that kids really related to Elmo. From that point, Sesame Street started a campaign to bring out Elmo through all of their wonderful licensing agreements. The popularity of Elmo hasn't stopped growing. In Kevin's own words:

> I've been performing Elmo for 13 years now. And I still find the response I get amazing. Especially when I do live shows across the country and come from behind the stage to see people and their reactions to me. They're like wow – he's black. It says something to white and black people alike: It can happen.

In addition to the phenomenal response that Kevin gets from performing Elmo, Kevin also gets to enjoy a portion of the commercial success that Elmo garners:

> Because of the *Tickle Me Elmo* doll, Elmo has gone to a whole new level. *Tickle Me Elmo* is the number one selling toy that's come through the Jim Henson Company and the Sesame Street Workshop. No other toy has done that well. However, I do not own this character. The Jim Henson Company does. I only perform the character. So, technically there were no rights that I really had to the character. However, Jim has given back one hundred percent. He has included me in the commercial benefits of Elmo.

So, don't be afraid to step out of the box. Box breakers are hand shakers, fortune takers, and decision-makers. Nobody but box breakers are worth talking about.

Master P

The Price of Success

"There's a cos' to be the boss!"

- Master P

What cost are you willing to pay to be the boss? What sacrifices are you willing to make to ensure that you get everything that you desire? Out of all the people I interviewed, not one of them stated that it would be an easy task. It only took one look in the intense eyes of these individuals to understand that hard work was the key to their achievements. Relentless and untiring hard work allowed these individuals to stretch to their maximum potential and to break the 'shackles' of self-limiting beliefs.

Best known for his "No Limit" approach in the hip-hop industry Percy Miller (a.k.a. Master P) has dazzled us all with his relentless pursuit of success.

Surprisingly, most people do not know the actual route traveled by Miller in order to achieve his fortune and fame.

Growing up in the projects in New Orleans, Miller had hoop dreams. He played basketball constantly, and hoped that he would be able to play in the NBA some day. After starring on the basketball team at Warren Eaton High School, Miller accepted a basketball scholarship from the University of Houston. A few weeks into living out his dreams, he suffered a knee injury and was sidelined. Hobbled by his bad knee, Miller set out for California at the age of 19 where he dabbled in the music industry. A year and a half later, in an attempt to salvage his basketball career, he enrolled at Merritt Junior College in Oakland. Discouraged by his on-going knee problems, Miller played briefly at Merritt College before deciding he would not pursue a career in basketball. He returned to his native Louisiana to focus on his music. That's when things began happening for Miller and they started happening fast.

At the tender age of 22, Miller devoted himself full-time to his music and by the age of 24, had established his record company, No Limit Records. No Limit began exuding force on the music industry. Miller's debut record, *The Ghetto is Trying to Kill Me*, sold over 100,000 copies; his second release, *99 Ways to Die*, sold 200,000; and his straight-to-video film, *I'm Bout it, Bout it* sold out at record stores around the U.S.

At the age of 26, impressed by Miller's business acumen, New Line Cinemas signed him to a multi-million dollar movie distribution deal. But, did he stop there? Of course not! The same year Miller released a string of platinum artists on his No Limit Records label. By the time the smoke had cleared (at the youthful age of twenty-eight), Miller's No Limit Records grossed a total of $56.5 million in 1998 alone - subsequently ranking him number ten in Forbes magazine's list of highest paid entertainers. His accomplishments were so phenomenal that he was also given the number one ranking on *The Source* magazine's Power 30 list of most influential people in the hip-hop industry. When asked, "What cost does he pay to be the boss?" Master P replied:

I pay a huge cost to be the boss. My work ethic is 24-7. I'm a early bird. And, the early bird gets the worm." He went on to add that, "Through my experiences, I have found that your character is judged by the lifestyle you live and the type of work ethic that you bring to the table. The harder you work – the more you get out of whatever you're putting in to. The problem with most people (particularly those who set million dollar goals) is that they want to see their goals happen overnight. It doesn't happen like that. You've got to have a dollar, then build up to ten dollars, then you build up to one hundred, then build up to ten thousand. The mistake that most people make is thinking they're not successful if they don't get the million. People need to understand that everyone has a growth period to go through. And, as long as you are constantly growing during this period – eventually, you will earn something. And whatever you are able to earn, you'll be able to hold on to forever. If you get something overnight, you'll lose it just as fast.

Straight from the mouth of the man himself, you can see there's a huge cost to be the boss.

So What You Gonna Do?

"It is through the practice of goal-setting that one can compensate for life's shortcomings, whether those shortcomings be real – lack of money, limited schooling, or poor self-image – or imagined."

- Dennis Kimbro,
Think and Grow Rich: A Black Choice

What steps are you going to take today to make your dreams a reality? There are people who routinely talk about what they are "about" to do or "fixin" to do, without ever actually doing anything. Ask yourself these questions, "Am I one of these people?" "Am I surrounded by people who only talk about doing things, but don't take actions to achieve those things?" If you answered "yes" to either or both of these questions, fix yourself on completing the following tasks:

1. Set specific goals and timelines for completing the various things you

want to accomplish in your life. Start with a goal for the year, then backtrack to decide what activities you need to accomplish each day to achieve that goal. Set goals that will benefit the financial, spiritual, physical, mental and emotional aspects of your life.

2. Allocate appropriate blocks of time in your days, weeks and months to accomplish each one of your goals.

3. Become crystal clear about what things are most important to you. Realize that life is not all about financial gain, and that a harmonious balance between all aspects of your life is what is ultimately desired.

4. Let go of past defeats, setbacks and failures. Instead of dwelling on the past, look to the future. Concentrate on developing the future you want to create.

5. Build meaningful relationships with people who share similar goals and objectives.
6. Recognize that time is on your side, so let go of the need to accomplish all of your goals immediately.

7. Stop planning and start doing. After you have laid the foundation for your plan, get started working towards accomplishing the goals you have set.

Not Allowing Your Minimums to Be Your Maximums

*"When you believe in something, you create a pathway for receiving it.
If you believe life is great, you see great possibilities, you plan for them and,
through your actions, you produce them. If you are doubtful and fearful, you
shun opportunities, you limp through life, and everything you touch turns to dust."*
- Susan L. Taylor, *Lesson in Living*

Just the other day, I was talking to my wife about her career aspirations. At the time, she had recently given birth to our second child and was actively seeking re-

Mara Brock-Akil

entry into the workplace. During her job search, we frequently talked about the various positions she was interested in pursuing. During our conversations, she would mention how she had refused a number of job offers because they did not meet her minimum annual salary requirements. Day after day, I witnessed her refuse jobs because the salary did not meet this standard.

Finally, after the fourth month of her search, she was offered a job at a local college awarding her the salary she was asking for - she immediately accepted. Satisfied, she made the comment, "Now I'm straight!" Unwisely and often times without proper professional guidance, many young, college-educated, African-Americans of all professions go through a similar process of accepting monetary offers for their professional services based upon parameters set during their college years. Bombarded by tons of information related to the salary ranges college graduates can expect from employers in the professional fields they intend to enter, these students established clearly set limits on their future market value. The most disturbing result of this programming is that these graduates willingly settle for these salaries without any detailed investigation of what their abilities are worth inside or outside of their professional field.

Young African-Americans, don't allow your minimums to be your maximums! Take time to fully investigate the maximum value that someone of equal or similar knowledge, experience, energy, skills and character is worth in all professions. Be objective and somewhat reasonable in your evaluation. Understand that with diligence, patience and creative thinking, you will actualize your maximum value.

A perfect example of a young, African-American woman who has maximized her value is Mara Brock-Akil, producer of the hit television shows, *Moesha* and *Girlfriends*. As one of only a handful of female, African-American producers in Hollywood, Mara is part of a new revolution of young black faces in Hollywood's decision-making hierarchy. However, Mara's value was not always maximized.

Mara's career started her freshman year at Northwestern University in Evanston, Illinois. Mara chose Northwestern because she has always wanted the best – and Northwestern had one of the best journalism departments in the country. She chose journalism as her major not because she really wanted to be a journalist, but because she loved to write and at the time journalism was the only way that she knew that a writer could earn a living. While at Northwestern, Mara was invited by her roommate's aunt to a Black Screenwriters Association meeting held in nearby Chicago. At the meeting, the guest speaker for the evening was Delle Chatman, a professor who taught screenwriting courses at Northwestern University. Coincidentally, Mara had unsuccessfully tried to get into Professor Chatman's classes for the past three years. After hearing Professor Chatman speak, Mara knew she wanted to become a screenwriter. She convinced Professor Chatman into allowing her to enroll into her class.

While taking her screenwriter courses, Mara became actively involved on-campus and was asked by fellow classmates and professors to write skits for several on-campus productions. Unknowingly, these assignments were preparing Mara for the career opportunities in which she would eventually attain success.

Although Mara appeared to be on the right track to success, she began working at a retail store after graduating from Northwestern instead of beginning her career as a screenwriter. Clearly not maximizing her value, unfulfilled and dissatisfied, Mara figured that if she was going to make it as a screenwriter she would have to be where screenwriters were. She followed her dreams and moved to Los Angeles.

In Los Angeles, Mara worked various odd jobs on different television sets. While on the set of *The Sinbad Show*, Mara befriended executive producer Ralph Farquhar, who eventually became her mentor. Farquhar (along with cocreators Sara Finney and Vida Spears) called Mara to inform her that they were creating a new television show, and they wanted to know if she would be interested in serving as a writer. Without hesitation, Mara replied "yes." She had seized her opportunity. Her outstanding performance as a writer, under the careful guidance of Sara Finney and Vida Spears, eventually led to Mara's promotion to producer. Mara began and is continuing to maximize her value.

Don't Start What You Can't Finish

"Men perish because they cannot join the beginning with the end."

- Unknown Author

A key factor in designing a success-filled life is adopting the practice to finish projects that you start. Before you make any personal commitments of your time and energy, develop a practice of considering the demands that the project being offered would require. First, ask specific questions about the project to determine if you are willing to fully commit. Second, decide what benefits could derive from the situation that could potentially create some future value in your life. Third, seek the advice of respected mentors to get their opinions about your proposed endeavor. However, do not let their opinions alone dictate your decision. Search deep inside yourself to discover if the opportunity is right for you; and make that the basis for your decision. If you determine that the project is not right for you, refuse to commit yourself to the project. Don't be afraid to say, "No." Developing these habits will ensure that you will become a results-oriented individual. Subsequently, you will discover that you will begin to develop a reputation as an outcome-oriented individual among your peers. This new reputation will lead you to opportunities you never dreamed possible. You will also find that results-oriented people are in high demand and will always have a position on somebody's team. Success will make it a habit of coming your way whether you like it or not.

LIVE LIFE!

Get Out and Make it Happen

"You need to git up, git out, and git somethin',
Don't let the days of your life pass by.
You need to git up, git out, and git somethin',
Don't spend all yo' time tryin' to git high.
You need to git up, git out, and git somethin',
How will you make it if you neva' even try?
You need to git up, git out, and git somethin',
Cuz you and I got to do for you and I."

— Outkast, *Git Up, Git Out*

"People who are victimized may not be responsible for being down, but they must be responsible for getting up…Change has always been led by those whose spirits were bigger than their circumstances."

— Jesse Jackson

Long ago in a small village, there lived four young men who loved riding their donkeys. They would ride their donkeys each day to a shady spot in the forest and brag about the type of straw they fed them. They would even brag about whose donkey was the most stubborn.

One day while sitting on their donkeys near the main road that went past their village, the young men noticed a group of strange men riding by in what looked like a steel drum with wheels. Soon, other vehicles followed. Some of the contraptions were small - some were large, but all were heading in the same direction. "Where are the men in the steel drums going?" one curious lad inquired. "I'm not sure," replied his friend, "but let's go find out." The young men set out on their donkeys to discover where the vehicles were heading.

After riding for several hours in search for the men in the trucks, the young men finally came to a remote part of the village. To their amazement, they discovered more than one thousand acres of their village's land fenced in by the strangers. Baffled by the sight, the young men approached and asked, "What are you gentlemen planning on doing with all this land?" The man responded, "We're starting a farm on one thousand acres of the richest land in this part of the world!" Stunned by his answer, the young men rode their donkeys back to the village to find out from the village chief what was going on.

After waiting for a brief period outside the chief's tent in hopes of a reasonable response, the chief emerged to inform the young men that he and the village elders had decided to rent the land to the men since the land was not being used. The young men could not believe what they were hearing. How could the chief and the village elders do such a thing without the entire village's consent? Months went by and the harvest season came. Still the young men sat on their donkeys. Day by day, the big vehicles drove past their village with loads of produce. The young men started to feel like they were being unjustly excluded from the abundant harvest being produced on "their land."

Determined to get their share of the benefits, they decided to visit the village chief again. "Can you somehow use your power to make the men in the vehicles pay a portion of their bounty to us since we are natives of the village?" the young men asked the chief. As they sat on their donkeys waiting for an answer, the chief told them something they would never forget. "Young men," he began, "Mother Earth only responds to the effort that you place into her. If you place no effort, you get no results." He went on to state that, "if you truly want an abundant harvest in life, you need to get off your 'asses' and make it happen." Are you like the young men on their donkeys waiting on your proverbial "ass" for your opportunities to happen? Do you think that your riches will somehow be given to you without any effort on your part? If you are able to gain your riches in this manner, consider yourself lucky – you will be part of the infinitesimally small number of individuals who achieve their success through accidental fortune. However, the majority of individuals who are successful do like the men in the trucks and uncover the hidden fortunes that exist around them. Always take the time to look for these treasures. Train yourself to look at things for what they could be, not for what they are. Don't be like the men on their donkeys waiting for good fortunes to come your way. If you do, you will forever be on the "outskirts" of success.

LIVE LIFE!

Get and Stay Married!!!

*"Marriage is a productive institution, not a consumer good. Marriage does not
simply certify existing loving relationships, but rather transforms the ways in
which couples act toward one another, toward their children,
and toward their future."*

- Steven Nock, *Marriage in Men's Lives*

Did you know that marriage is, has and will continue to be one of the most
fundamental keys to success? Look closely around you and you will discover
that the majority of emotionally stable, financially secure and socially well-
adjusted people have embraced the institution of marriage. This does not mean
that marriage is always beneficial or that success is impossible without it; but,
when you look at percentages, healthy and committed marriages have been the
vehicles that have assisted a large number of people in creating success for
themselves and their families. Obviously, you have to get married to the right
kind of person that you love with the right values. A person who:

1. Puts God and family first.

2. Centers their actions around meeting the family's needs first, then their
needs second.

3. Does whatever is required to maintain the stability of the family (i.e.
working two jobs while their spouse goes to school, leveraging family
credit to invest in a business).

4. Realizes that the frivolous use of economic resources negatively impacts
the family and threatens its livelihood. For those who enter into a marriage with the above items incorporated into their mindsets, they often
reap many of the rewards that marriage offers. These benefits include:

• Increased family and personal wealth.

• Longer and healthier life spans of members
(particularly husbands).

• Increased well-being of children in the marriage.

The reasons for the benefits listed above are attributed to specific elements contained within a marriage. From a financial prospective, individuals who are married often exhibit higher levels of wealth than single people do in similar age and income brackets. Why? The answer is twofold. First, marriage creates greater economies of scale. Just as the case of an apartment renter who wants to find a roommate to cut his/her expenses in half (i.e. rent and utility bills), the same holds true in a marriage where the sharing of household goods and chores creates greater economic efficiencies. In addition, marriage creates economies of scale through the combining of emotional and financial resources of the couple's families. It is not uncommon for parents and other relatives to contribute resources of all kinds (i.e. baby clothes, monetary gifts, household appliances, etc.) to the marriage; thereby, reducing many of the financial burdens experienced by single individuals. Second, marriage leads to increased wealth from productivity gained in the division of household responsibilities. For example, people who live alone are typically responsible for all aspects of their lives (i.e. job related work, paying bills, preparing meals, washing clothes, etc.). However, people who are married can divide these day-to-day activities leaving extra time to devote to additional meaningful activities in their lives (i.e. exercising, reading, etc).

Other benefits that marriages provide are longer and healthier life spans for spouses and increased states of well being for children. Studies have shown increases in the life expectancies and the emotional health of married men and women compared to their divorced and never-married counterparts. Wives, particularly, encourage husbands to seek medical advice when health problems begin to occur. For spouses, marriage also offers the highly sought after companionship and friendship that humans seek to achieve. Someone to share your intimate thoughts and lucrative ideas without fear that they may be stolen or ridiculed. True companions nurture and challenge while providing encouragement for a better outcome in any situation. Marriage allows children to draw from the emotional, financial and spiritual accounts of both parents giving them greater opportunities for success. It is in such an environment that children learn to love one another like they love themselves and are hence able to become loving and responsible adults as they escape the spiritual decadence and emotional distress that other environments may foster.

Ultimately, people need to understand that marriage is a life-long commitment. Honor your spouse and love and care for him/her and understand that you are committed to a lifetime partnership. Learn about finances. Learn how to fight fairly and learn that arguments and disagreements are not uncommon events in any marriage. Be strong and secure in your Faith and commitment to God and your marriage. If you do, you will be able to see obstacles in your marriage for what they really are, destroyers of love and happiness.

Controlling Careless Consumption

Consumption is defined as the act or process of consuming goods and services by use, waste, decay or destruction. As a young African-American striving for success, you must give careful consideration to the amount of goods and services that you consume. Begin thinking of yourself and your household as a tightly ran business. As the owner of your business, would you want your employees carelessly giving away products purchased by your business; ordering more products than needed; and/or spending large quantities of time on unproductive activities? Of course not! Because as the owner, you know that these actions are detrimental to your business; and, could ultimately lead to its failure. Think of your personal consumption patterns in this manner, also.

There are five main categories of consumption you need to control to be successful:

- Food
- Utilities
- Clothing
- Addictive Substances & Behaviors, and
- Personal Finances

From my research, these categories represent the main areas most young people have difficulties with and need to ultimately master. To give you a better idea for controlling and effectively managing your personal consumption habits, I have included a list of tips in these (5) five major categories for your use.

Food

1. Package all leftovers in containers. Food does not spoil as fast when stored in a container.

2. Note the expiration dates on perishable items. Use items that are scheduled to expire first.

3. Cook enough at dinner to make lunch for the next day. As you prepare your dinner plate, have containers available so you can prepare lunch, too. This technique eliminates spending enormous amounts of money on eating out.

4. Eat leftovers.

5. Buy in bulk.

6. Discipline yourself to take advantage of coupons and mail-in rebates for items you normally buy. Use a portion of your time while you are at work or at home to organize your coupons and mail-in rebates.

Utilities

1. Make sure your house/apartment is properly insulated. A poorly insulated residence will lead to higher utility bills.

2. During winter months, wear appropriate clothing (i.e. a coat or a jacket) while you are inside your home. This prevents you from over-using your heat. Wearing heavy clothing inside may not be comfortable or convenient, but it is cost-effective.

3. Carry only basic telephone service. Eliminate additional features like call waiting and caller identification.

4. Use pre-paid calling cards at home for long distance calls. This allows you to moni-

tor your long distance call usage.

Clothing

1. Develop relationships with people who hyper-consume clothes (particularly if you have children). Wait until they get rid of clothes that they or their children no longer use. This will allow you to wear high quality items at no cost.

2. De-sensitize yourself to the words "sale" and "clearance." Department stores have realized for years that they can cajole shoppers into buying by using "sale" or "clearance" in their advertising (i.e. One-Day Sale, Spring Clearance). Only use sales or clearances to purchase items you have been waiting to drop in price.

3. Shop at thrift stores, discount outlets, or consignment stores.

Addictive Substances

1. Eliminate using all addictive substances (i.e. cigarettes, alcohol, illegal drugs, etc.). Not only do these substances lead to the financial destruction of people who regularly abuse them, they do considerable harm to the physical, emotional and spiritual aspects of a person's life.

2. Remove all addictive substances from your household. The less convenient they are to access, the better.

3. Encourage having house/apartment parties instead of patronizing nightclubs. This will substantially reduce your entertainment costs.

Personal Finances

Use the following "Ten Basic Rules of Money Management" provided by the Consumer Credit Counseling Service (CCCS) to determine how to get your personal finances under control.

1. PLAN – Plan for the future, major purchases and periodic expenses.

2. SET FINANCIAL GOALS – Determine short and long-term financial goals.

3. KNOW YOUR FINANCIAL SITUATION – Determine monthly living expenses, periodic expenses and monthly debt payments. Compare expenses to monthly net income. Be aware of your total indebtedness.

4. DEVELOP A REALISTIC SPENDING PLAN – Follow your budget as closely as possible. Evaluate your budget. Compare actual expenses with planned expenses.

5. DON'T ALLOW EXPENSES TO EXCEED INCOME – Avoid paying only the minimum on your charge cards. Don't charge more every month than you are repaying to your creditors.

6. SAVE – Save for periodic expenses, such as car and home maintenance. Save 5 to 10% of your net income. Accumulate 3 to 6 months' salary in an emergency fund.

7. PAY YOUR BILLS ON TIME – Maintain a good credit rating. If you are unable to pay your bills as agreed, contact your creditors and explain your situation. **Contact Consumer Credit Counseling Service** for professional advice.

8. DETERMINE THE DIFFERENCE BETWEEN WANTS AND NEEDS – Take care of your needs first. Money should be spent for wants only after needs have been met.

9. USE CREDIT WISELY – Use credit for safety, convenience, and planned purchases. Determine the total you can comfortably afford to purchase on

credit. Don't allow your credit payments to exceed 20% of your net income. Avoid borrowing from one creditor to pay another.

10. KEEP A RECORD OF DAILY EXPENDITURES – Be aware of where your money is going. Use a spending diary to assist you in identifying areas where adjustments need to be made.

Malcolm K. Berkley

Are You Willing to Bear the Burden?

"The burden of being Black is that you have to be superior just to be equal. But the glory of it is that, once you achieve, you have achieved, indeed."

- Jesse Jackson

Blessed are those who have accepted the responsibility placed on them by the Creator to love, serve and protect all human beings that inhabit this Earth. A responsibility many have chosen to avoid becoming a failure in God's sight. So, the question becomes will you take your share of the load and carry the weight present in your household, family and community? Will you be there when the going gets tough? Or will you duck-and-dodge and get going like those absentee mothers and fathers who abandon their families for lives of drug abuse and crime? Or better yet, will you be like those ducking-and-dodging spouses that pack-up and run instead of staying and working things out when family finances get tight or when relationships become strained? Or even worse, will you be like that ducking-and-dodging friend who finds a way to disappear when fame or fortunes are lost? If you are not willing to bear the burden and make the bleak situations you're faced with better, stop reading this book – success is not what you're looking for. Go buy and read *Tales of the Coward* by Runaway Chicken. He's got what you need. Simply put, bite down and bear the burden! Those who carry the burden reap the rewards. Burden bearers are people who force themselves to confront their obstacles head on. And as a result, build an insurmountable base of character and strength when they work through and eliminate their problems. Burden evaders are the opposite of burden bearers. Burden evaders avoid carrying their loads creating lives that lack substance and structure. Do not let yourself be tricked by the life of the burden evader thinking they get more in the end. What initially appear to be gains for the burden evader like having less responsibility, more time for him/herself, or less money spent are often pitfalls that lead them deeper in the holes of vainness, immaturity and misdirection. Be a true burden bearer like Malcolm K. Berkley – Public Relations Director at United Parcel Services (UPS), who was forced at a young age to understand the responsibility but ultimately received the gift from bearing heavy burdens.

Born the first of two children to a young mother (16 years old) and a young father (22 years old), Malcolm grew up in a flat-out poor, not even working poor section of Harlem. Drug use was all around him. Crime was all around him. All of the dysfunctional things of ghetto life were around him. Although life outside his home was rough, life inside the doors of the Berkley household was totally different. As Malcolm describes it, "If the Huxtables were the perfect family as far as being fun, loving and functional - take the material things, class and status out of the picture – so were we." Despite all the other things that his family had to deal with, home was always home and things were always "straight" at home. Even when things were bad, home was good. Even when his mother couldn't eat, she made sure home stayed together. Even when he was sleeping on a mattress standing on paint cans and the family's government assistance and welfare checks didn't come in, the Berkley's were "straight:

It's funny because it taught me at a young age that you don't need all the things you put your hands on and possess to be happy. Happiness to me isn't tied to a dollar amount or some material possession. It depends on how strong the family is.

The Berkley's stayed strong and managed until tragedy struck the household. Malcolm was 10 years old. His younger sister was seven. In Malcolm's own words:

My father had really high expectations of himself and he couldn't necessarily meet those (expectations). So, rather than be a failure or what he perceived as being a failure, he decided to leave us. But in leaving us, he planted so many seeds in my sister, my mom and myself that to this day he still lives. We're living and doing based on the things that he said to us. It's eerie almost because the night that my pops died, the movie Mahogany was on. It was a late movie and was scheduled to be on until 10:00 p.m. So when he came in about 8:30 p.m., mom started telling us that it was time to go to bed. To our surprise, he was like 'no' let them stay up, which was strange because we had to be in bed at 9:00 p.m. every night. But on this particular night, we were allowed to stay up at his command. So, we watched the movie. And after the movie was over, he spent an extra long period of time in my sister's room just with her. Put her in bed. Talked to her. Did whatever he had to do. Then, he came over to my room. And it's funny because we talked about a lot of stuff. For 10 years old, we talked about a lot of things. But, the last thing he said to me before I went to sleep, before he left the room, was always take care of your mother and sister and get your education. Those were his last words. Then, he kissed me on my head and left the room. I woke up around 4 or 5 o'clock in the morning to find my grandparents there (in the apartment). My uncles were downstairs. Apparently, whatever happened – happened. And, my sister and I slept through the whole thing. And, it's not a big apartment. But we slept through the paramedics coming in trying to revive (him). We slept through my mom losing it. We slept through all of that. When people talk about spirituality and all those other things, I really understand that because I firmly believe that it was his love that allowed us not to wake up in that traumatic and tragic scene. And again, he said some things to my sister that she still won't share with me. And it was one of those things. He knew what he was going to do. And those last words that he said that last hour he spent with each of us meant something.

Life moved on. But, things changed drastically in the Berkley household:

I remember it like it happened yesterday. Going through that at 10 years old and now, all of a sudden, ordained the man of the house. I got a younger sister and a mother and I'm now the man of the household. So the whole self-reliant, self-sufficient message that has always been preached to me now becomes even more important because I've got to be strong. Over the years, a step-pop comes into the picture. I'm a teenager/young man now. Money becomes something that I'm always looking to make. Always driven. Success wasn't even a question. It was a given. There was no question.

Malcolm was lucky. By God's Grace, he managed not to get caught up in New York street life and graduated from high school. He decided to attend school at Morehouse College in Atlanta, Georgia. "Morehouse was a lot of fun. It was a lot of work." After attending Morehouse for two years, Malcolm realized that he lost some of his focus, so he left. He went back to New York to help start a company as a promoter that ultimately changed his life. Although he was making money and having fun as a New York promoter, Malcolm was committed to remaining true to his father's wish for him to get his education and his goal to get his college degree from Morehouse. So, he returned to Morehouse two years later and obtained his Bachelor of Arts degree in English.

So how was Malcolm able to bear the burden of growing up impoverished as a child in Harlem, of dealing with the pain and trauma associated with his father's untimely death and of the premature duty placed on him to take care of his mother and sister and to get his education? Malcolm looked at the situation then and continues to see things this way:

> If it ain't rough, it ain't right! For those who don't know, that's a hook from an old hip hop song back in the late 70's or early 80's. I probably say it to myself at least once a day. When the stinky stuff hits the fan, I'll say it. I'll also say it to people going through their own trials and tribulations. If it's too easy, something is wrong. And it just fits. Because all my life I've had to overcome something and those around me have had to overcome something. So, don't become discouraged when things get rough. Look at it as an opportunity or a challenge to help you succeed. And I firmly believe that you learn more from what goes wrong than what goes right. So, for me if it ain't rough (if you open too many doors for me), I'm going to tell you to stop because it ain't supposed to be that easy. If you have it that easy, ultimately you lose appreciation for what you have. 'Power concedes no demand without a struggle.' That's a quote from the great Frederick Douglass. So, this ain't nothing new. He could have said, 'if it ain't rough, it ain't right' and it would've meant the same thing. So, that's my motto and I don't plan on changing that.

Rev. Jamal Harrison-Bryant

The Power of Galvanizing

"Galvanize – The unique ability to gather people of like minds and visions to accomplish well-defined tasks and/or objectives."

- Unknown Author

Analyze the lives of successful people and you will discover this ability present. Whether it be the ability to mobilize large groups of people (like Dr. Martin Luther King, Jr. during the March on Washington and Minister Louis

Farrakhan during the Million Man March) or small groups of people like a neighborhood watch committee – galvanizing is another tool you will find present in the work chest of successful men and women. Learning and using the power of galvanizing gives many successful African-Americans the opportunity to reach positions of influence and prominence at a young age. Consider Rev. Jamal Harrison-Bryant, former National Youth and College Director of the National Association for the Advancement of Colored People (NAACP). By the age of 28, Rev. Bryant had actively participated in the 1994 elections in South Africa that officially ended apartheid and elected Nelson Mandela as president. He also participated in the 1998 Million Youth March here in the U.S. Currently, he serves as founder and pastor of Empowerment Temple Church in Baltimore, Maryland. Rev. Bryant has discovered that great things happen when you bring together people to affect change.

Although Rev. Bryant understands the power of galvanizing now, this was not always the case. During his stay in South Africa working with the African National Congress (ANC), Rev. Bryant was touched by the sight of tens of thousands of people going to the polling stations as early as four o'clock in the morning to vote for the first time – officially ending apartheid. This experience challenged him to eradicate the apathy that he believed existed within the African-American community, particularly among young people - an apathy he was all to familiar with growing up as a young man in Baltimore. Although he was the son of a well-known and highly-respected preacher and the first of two children born in a prominent Christian family, Rev. Bryant found himself succumbing to the pressures running reckless among Baltimore's delinquent youth. As a result, he failed the eleventh grade. Rev. Bryant was scheduled to repeat his junior year, but because his father's jurisdiction covered churches in West Africa, his family moved to Liberia.

In Liberia, Rev. Bryant resumed his schooling at the American Cooperative School (ACS) – a school where the children of diplomats from over 47 nations attended school. Rev. Bryant was surprised to find out that everyone at ACS was focused on achieving excellence and being smart, whereas in Baltimore, it was not cool to do well in school. This school culture encouraged him to do better. In addition, Rev. Bryant's stay in Liberia – a free African country with a Black president and a Black mayor with Black people living without being subjugated - inspired him to believe that African-Americans were capable of accomplishing these things as well.

Upon returning to the States, Rev. Bryant passed his GED exams and was accepted into Morehouse College the same year. At Morehouse, he was able to cultivate his leadership abilities further from his continuous exposure to other African-American men who understood the power of galvanizing like then U.S. Secretary of Commerce Ron Brown, former Atlanta mayor Maynard Jackson and prominent Detroit, Michigan pastor Charles Adams. Rev. Bryant has been moving and galvanizing ever since. He went on to get his master's degree in Divinity from Duke University, then soon after graduating, was asked by President & CEO of the NAACP, Mr. Kweisi Mfume, to serve as Director of the NAACP's National Youth and College Department. It was Rev. Bryant's gift for galvanizing that prompted Mr. Mfume to hire Rev. Bryant for the position. Rev. Bryant's job at the NAACP allowed him to mobilize youth organizations in the southeastern U.S. during the Million Youth March. It is also his gift of galvanizing that allows Rev. Bryant to successfully pastor his church in Baltimore, Maryland. In Rev. Bryant's own words, "Mobilizing is a call to action; it is the power to effectuate change among people. The only way that true change takes place is through galvanizing people."

Respect individuals like Rev. Bryant for the influence they possess. However, realize that the ability to galvanize is a skill that you can acquire. First, begin by giving your time, energy and resources to people in need of your abilities. Second, work on developing the trust and respect of others who possess or are striving to achieve influence. Third, attach yourself to a cause, belief or purpose. Taking these actions will ensure your place in what I term the C.O.G. (circle of galvanization). Once you are in this circle, galvanizing will become an ongoing reality of your existence.

John Singleton

The Power of Production

"In this world, there are consumers and producers – What side are you on?
- Unknown Author

*"P, look around man! Do you see what I see? I see money. Look at my man over there
selling T-shirts. Brotha over there selling pies and papers. Tape man over there.
Everybody's moving making money, right? ...while we standing still being broke! I
figured all this out man. All this! This whole world moves forward through transac-
tions. Commerce!! The exchange of goods and services. All the real ballers and suc-*

cessful folks are sellers. And all the broke people playing catch up are buyers. I ain't trying to go out like that P. I'm a be a seller. I'm gon' get my own business. And change the game."

- Tyrese Gibson as Jodie, *Baby Boy*

A fundamental key to success is possessing the ability to produce. Without the capacity of production, an idea or project never gets completed. Given the nature of humans, people naturally want to do and want to create more with their lives. To aspire is good, it's natural, it's a beginning step of achievement. However, there are those aspiring individuals that do not commit themselves to the production process; therefore, failing to achieve the results of their aspirations. They have the passion to speak on and convey their thoughts to others, yet between the excitement of the thought and the actual achievement of the idea, something gets lost. It is between the thought and the achievement where the key to production lies.

Webster defines production as the creation of goods and services from inputs or resources. When a company such as Ford makes a truck or car or when Exxon refines a gallon of gasoline, the activity is production. The same is true for doctors who produce medical services, teachers who produce educational lessons, and singers who produce entertainment. However, production is much more involved than the simple manufacturing of a product or service. Production also involves a distinct set of skills and abilities that people who are efficient in the art of production are able to understand and execute well. First, effective producers are leaders who constantly work at bettering their production goals and hold themselves accountable when their goals are not met. Second, efficient producers (whether as individual workers or overseers of producing entities) are committed to developing the fastest, least expensive, highest quality good or service they can produce with the resources they have available. These individuals understand and value time, money and quality and work diligently to make sure that each are used and maximized properly. These proficient producers (particularly those mentioned above who supervise producing entities) are aware of the fact that people, whether as investors or consumers, are concerned with all three and how all three impact their lives.

A good example of the power involved in production can be found in an analysis of the movie-making process. Movie producers, in particular, have the major responsibility of making things happen by acting as intermediaries between directors, investors, actors, and writers. They have to ensure that the production of their film is accomplished within a defined budget, a specific period of time and with an anticipated level of quality.

Look at the accomplishments of movie producer extraordinaire John Singleton, who by the age of thirty-two has produced a staggering six motion pictures (*Boyz N the Hood* – 1991, *Poetic Justice* – 1993, *Higher Learning* – 1995, *Rosewood* – 1997, *Shaft* – 2000, *Baby Boy* – 2001) in a span of ten, short years - grossing an estimated $250 million dollars world-wide at the box-office. John's phenomenal ability to write, direct and produce movies has gained him widespread acclaim and garnered him two Oscar nominations: one for Best Original Screenplay and the other for Best Director – making him the first African-American and the youngest person to be nominated for the latter honor. John has also been credited for bringing to light many social issues such as gang violence, racial injustice, and ghetto life and love in an entertaining and realistic way. However, in order for John to reach the level he has achieved as a movie producer, he had to first tap into the spirit of enterprise and hustle ingrained in him as a result of his South Central Los Angeles upbringing and set out to acquire the skills he needed to make movies. John states:

> I think that I was bred to do what I do. Although I grew up in South Central Los Angeles, I spent a lot of time getting on the bus, going to the library, and reading about film and art. I got on the bus and went up to Hollywood to check out movies. I basically lived, breathed, and ate this thing for many years before I made my first film at twenty-two. I made my first film at a very young age. But, I did a whole lot before then.

After John learned the art of Hollywood filmmaking that allowed him to make his first movie *Boyz N the Hood*, he continued to make things happen by duplicating these same movie-making processes to create his next five movies. In John's own words, he states his process for producing movies:

> I find the product. I find the story or book that can be made into a movie; or I sit down and write the script; or find the writer that can write the film. After finding the story, everything comes from there. I get it hooked up with a studio and then I cast it. I find the actor. If I can't get a star to do the movie because I

can't afford to pay a star a lot of money, I make a star. I find someone with natural talent who is just getting into the business that I believe is going to be watchable enough to be on the screen.

As John has evolved in his film-production process, he has also learned some interesting things about the movie-making business as a whole. He's discovered that: "Once you get in the game, the hardest thing becomes staying in the game. Staying in the game means getting yourself endorsed and then building up a reputation to be taken seriously in this business." Through his emergence as a leader in the film industry, John has proven by example the power of production. John has mastered the ability to put small components together that make the big picture happen. Well aware of his power to produce, John asserts: "I make things happen. There's power in being able to make things happen." So, don't play – produce!! Work hard at becoming proficient in producing individually and with other people as a unit.

Other Keys To Mastering the Power of Production

In your pursuit for better production processes, keep the following points in mind:

1. Always start out with the end in mind. Visualize what it is that you ultimately want to achieve.

2. Make sure everyone involved understands the vision/goal you are going after. If people don't understand what it is you desire, they can't assist you on your journey. The onus is on you to make your vision clear.

3. Plan all tasks and activities needed to get your objective accomplished. Start your planning process by attempting to identify successful models already laid out for achieving your desired task. Don't reinvent the wheel if you don't have to. Use the success formulas of others who have accomplished similar objectives. Next, write down everything that you need to do to reach your desired goal. Remember: If you don't write it down, it doesn't get done.

4. Establish deadlines for completion of these tasks. What needs to be done first, second, and so on? How long will each task take realistically for you to complete? A good rule of thumb is to condition yourself to complete the tasks that you don't want to do or don't like or know how to do first. Conditioning yourself to accomplish these tasks is a great method to prevent complacency, procrastination and/or avoidance of critical tasks.

5. Project tangible results (i.e. attendance numbers, financial gains, weight loss, and etc.) and intangible results (i.e. better client/network relations, better image, and etc.) you expect to experience from your proposed endeavor.

6. Carry out each of your planned tasks and activities until your objective is met. When carrying out your plan, work at adopting the following skills and perspectives in order to become an effective executor of your tasks:

- Organize and schedule your time and effort wisely. This includes developing the ability to multi-task (working on more than one project at a time).
- Understand and become good at developing and meeting budget costs.
- Be flexible. Everything will not happen when and how you want it.
- Stay hungry and motivated. Perseverance and endurance are the keys to your success.

7. Once you've achieved your goals, take time to reflect and celebrate your accomplishments. Life is good when you accomplish your goals.

8. Set new goals. Don't allow the accomplishment of your previous goals to create complacency in your life. Move on, stay focused and work towards the new objectives you have established.

Laila Ali

Champions Never Take The Easy Way Out – Pay the Price

"Good things are golden. They don't come cheap. Therefore, there's going to be a huge price to pay to get them. The cost is not always money. The price is paid by your level of patience and perseverance, time and energy."
- Sonya Tate, Educator

When you think of a champion, you think of the best - the greatest – the one that paid the ultimate price. You think of the one that worked harder, longer and better than their competitors. One that has excelled and prevailed. A champion is the one that is conceived with desire; raised carefully under the strong hands of sacrifice and determination; and matured gracefully by the spirit of solidarity to become…a champion.

Although the word champion is usually reserved for athletes, it can be applied to anyone. Doctors, teachers, business owners and parents all have the potential to be champions, for their make-ups are the same. Their final products are the difference.

However, not all people involved in these professions espouse the level of love, give up all the things required, or go the extra steps needed to be a champ. True champions adopt these critical characteristics to reach the final stage of personal success. Laila Ali, daughter of boxing legend Muhammad Ali, is a prime example of a true champion. First, she started her quest in women's boxing with an insatiable desire to conquer the sport. A desire to do and be the best:

> The first thing that happened to me was I got this feeling that made me want to do it (box). So it wasn't like I said, 'I think I want to box' like it just popped in my head out of nowhere. I saw it on TV, and then I got a burning desire to want it bad enough to work on it everyday.

Second, Laila relinquished many of the loves and freedoms of other women her age to reach her goal. For her, this meant giving up weekends at the clubs and fattening foods for arduous practices, tight schedules, and strict diets:

> The training and sacrifices that I go through to be a fighter is nothing special. It's what you have to do to box. No matter what, you can't be out late partying, hanging-out, spending your time all week thinking about what you're going to wear this weekend to the club. I don't allow myself to have those types of thoughts. I don't want them… The other things that I have to sacrifice are the things I like to eat. Put it like this, I don't eat fried food. I don't eat junk food like potato chips, ice cream – junk – stuff you can just go in the store and pick up. For the most part, I don't eat to satisfy my hunger. I eat to give my body nutrition. So, I'm not just sitting down to enjoy my food. I'm sitting down to nourish my body.

Third, she sustains her level of sacrifice with unwavering determination to make it through difficult times:

Life is difficult for me. When I say difficult, I don't mean that in a negative way. It's just not something that's easy... When you want certain things and you believe in certain things and stand for certain things, sometimes things don't go your way. But, you're going to still keep striving until you get what you want. And that makes it difficult.

And last, Laila has patiently and persistently gained the necessary boxing skills and fight experience needed to be considered one of boxing's "greats." However, Laila's true measure of greatness will not come from her accomplishments as a boxer alone. Laila, as well as all true champions, understand that greatness doesn't just come from belts or titles – it comes from a spirit. A spirit that connects those unique individuals, who became champions professionally and personally, back to the sources from which their successes come. A spirit of solidarity, love, and humility that reminds individuals that they did not make it alone and that their accomplishments were gained by efforts greater than one. So, be like Laila and embark on your journey to greatness, but know you are going to have to pay the price. As Laila puts it:

If being a champion was easy, then everybody would do it

Laila reminds herself of this fact when she's running, the day of a fight, or when she's looking in the ice cream store. And she applies it to anything:

If getting in shape was easy, then everybody would be in shape. If running was easy, then everybody would be out running. If being a champ was easy, everybody would be a champ. But, it's only those certain ones that are willing to pay the price to get ahead.

The Inspiration: Bringing Forth What's Within to Create Young, Black Success

Alonzo Mourning

Listen to Your Spirit

"There is a sacred place within us where wisdom and clarity dwell. This is where God resides and has being. This is the simple truth we were born to discover. Awakened to this truth, we won't fear the darkness of the night."

- Susan L. Taylor, *Lessons in Living*

Have you noticed that the latest trend for self-improvement seems to be getting in touch with your spirit? Throughout our country, people of influence (from walks of life other than the religious community) are talking about the human spirit and how the development or demise of it impacts your life. For example, talk show host Oprah

Winfrey and award-winning author Iyanla Vanzant are addressing the subject of spirituality extensively in their respective arenas. These women are showing people how to rely on their spirits when battling personal issues regarding love, life, and money. Sensing people's desires to create and maintain balanced lives, these women have made it popular through television, print, and audio for other people to talk about their spirituality. Even men like singer/songwriter, Lenny Kravitz, and basketball star, Alonzo Mourning, have credited spirituality for pulling them through difficult times. However, the concept of spirituality and its effect on people's lives is not new and has always played a significant part in the history of the Black community constantly reminding African-Americans who they are. This fact becomes apparent through the many African-American adages that refer to the spirit. Sayings like: "She was filled with the spirit in church today" or "that man has a mean spirit about him" have always been part of African-American culture. The power of the African-American spirit was the critical factor that allowed many to stand tall and remain strong when faced with life's most historical atrocities. Remember that your spirit is always there. It is omniscient - transcending all cultures, ages, genders, races, and religions.

Your spirit ultimately tells you what are the right and wrong things to do in situations that you are faced with. It's your inner voice - the voice of reason. It's the place where you will ultimately find inner peace. Peace within yourself. Peace with your surroundings. Peace with your family, friends and neighbors. It's the place where the core goodness of man resides. And it is at that core where each individual has to bring his/her soul to rest if it is ever going to be at ease. Don't fight this spirit. Flow with it. Let it consume your thoughts, words and actions. By doing so, your actions will operate in a manner that is consistent with the true essence of yourself. You will find comfort knowing that you are behaving in a way that is in alignment with the type of person you were created to be. By constantly choosing to ignore this spirit, you will be plagued with inner conflicts that will corrupt your soul and disease your conscious and subconscious mind. People who consistently ignore their spirits live in what some call a "Hell on Earth" - the end of the downward spiral of self-deprecating behavior. Hell on Earth is a place where young African Americans (whether admittedly through their testimonies or plainly demonstrated through their reckless actions) have lived. Young African-Americans like Darryl Strawberry (former player with the New York Mets), Bobby Brown (former member of R&B group New Edition),

R&B artist Mary J. Blige, and Todd Bridges (former star of television sitcom Different Strokes) to name a few have at one time or another lived out some form of Hell on Earth. For some, Hell on Earth was one or a combination of drug abuse, alcohol abuse and promiscuity that guided them to their unfortunate circumstances. Initially, these individuals locked themselves in this hellish prison with the key of their unresolved issues. Their behavior became the prison guards to the emotional and mental states of distress they were living. They were not in balance. Their lives were not harmonious and it showed. Some chose to ignore their spirit because they were not in touch with it. Others just chose not to listen. Some simply lacked faith that what the spirit was telling them was the right thing for them to do. For your family, friends and loved ones, don't allow yourself to fall into this trap. Let your spirit be your guide and success will follow. Although not faced with the circumstances faced by the individuals discussed above, read how Alonzo Mourning, professional basketball player, talked about how his spirit helped to guide him through a difficult battle he faced with kidney disease:

> The one thing that was key in this whole process (recovering from kidney disease) was that I knew my mind and my spirit was healthy. It was just the shell that God had given me – my body – was a little out of whack. And it was just a matter of time, time being the essence here, that my body would catch up to my mind and my spirit. Everybody has a spirit. When you die, your body goes in the ground. But, your spirit lives on. Your spirit goes somewhere else. The shell that was given to you stops working. That goes in the ground. That turns back to dust. But your overall makeup, your spirit, who you are as a person, what you believe in. That's your spirit. My spirit talks to me. My spirit is a part of who I am. It's my subconscious. My body was telling me, 'Hey, you're struggling.' But, I knew that my body had a memory. That it remembered how it used to be. So, it will be just a matter of time before my body will get back to that stage again. My body just has some miles on it. And it's just a matter of me taking a different approach in taking care of it. But, as long as I keep my spirit, my mind and my heart strong then it's only a matter of time that my body is going to catch up.

That's the power of the spirit.

Values Versus Dollars

For the love of money
People will steal from their mother
For the love of money
People will rob their own brother
For the love of money
People can't even walk the street
Because they never know who in the world they're gonna beat
For that lean, mean, mean green
Almighty dollar,
For the love of money
All for the love of money
Don't let, don't let, don't let money rule you
For the love of money

- - The O'Jays, *For The Love Of Money.*

In America, people often associate success with money. Let's be frank, nobody wants to be broke. If you work hard, you want to be compensated for your efforts. There is nothing wrong with wanting money or with having financial success as goals. The problem arises when a person is willing to do anything for money; even when it goes against his or her own values. You can have all the money and approval in the world, but if you are not doing what's right, then you are not successful.

Over the years, young African-Americans have witnessed a few rising stars who have transformed their lifestyles because they realized that their way of earning a living did not agree with their fundamental values. These courageous individuals changed course in the middle of their careers (a decision most people would not make, especially while their earning potentials were rising). However, James Green a.k.a. "Woody" from the R&B Group Dru Hill and Mason Betha a.k.a. "Mase" former Bad Boy Entertainment recording artist made the decision to align their lives closer to the principles they believed were right.

Both were forecasted to have long and prosperous professions entertaining their fans with the R&B and hip-hop music they promoted. However, something within them did not believe that the actions they were taking were right. In order to continue exercising their God-given abilities without compromising their entrenched values, it meant for Woody leaving Dru Hill to record a gospel album. And for Mase, it meant leaving the rap business, returning to school, and ministering to those in need.

There is an important lesson to be gained from their examples. As you have heard before, money isn't everything. Doing what you feel and believe is right - is! Another example of an individual who transformed his life and decided to do the right thing is Deion Sanders, former professional football player and major league baseball star. Deion decided that the only right choice for him was salvation in the eyes of the Lord.

Deion Sanders has always had a strong work ethic and a strong desire to do the right thing. Even from the beginning of his professional football career, he always used to talk to his teammates about doing what's right – not drinking, not smoking, staying straight, doing their best in practice, and always going to the higher expectancy level. His teammates listened to him because he was doing it himself - on the field and off. At least that's what they thought. Deion had private issues with infidelity and sexual promiscuity. However, Deion wasn't completely corrupt. He's never smoked cigarettes, used illegal drugs, or tasted the likes of alcohol. Deion's foremost problem as he describes it in his autobiography *Power, Money, & Sex: How Success Almost Ruined My Life* was that he wasn't plugged into the Source:

> Everything needs a power source. The reason the light comes on when you walk into a room and flip on the switch is because there's a power source. If you take away the supply of power, the light can do nothing. It's useless. It has absolutely no power in and of itself. But men and women need power, too, and the only way they can have it is through a relationship with something or someone powerful (pp.131- 132).

Deion longed to be plugged in. He had a longtime habit of reading a verse of scripture from the Bible every day. Even before he was delivered, he realized that there was something in that book that he needed to hear. It wasn't that Deion was super religious, he only had a superficial awareness of biblical teachings at the time. Deion just knew that he needed God in his life, but he wasn't quite sure how to get there:

> There was a time when I wouldn't play a game on Sunday in the NFL unless I was wearing my cross chain…I was so naïve about spirituality at that time that I thought I had to play with the Lord around my neck, like I had Him on a chain! So I played every game with that chain hanging around my neck… I always knew I needed a relationship with God. My mother and grandmother made sure I understood that I needed God in my life. But I wasn't living it. I just didn't know how to make the move to the next level (pp.109-110).

Deion tried everything to get to that next level of fulfillment. He tried parties, women, buying expensive jewelry, cars and gadgets; but nothing helped. There was no peace. Finally, after two failed suicide attempts and the painful realization that there was more to life than power, money and sex, Deion came to the understanding that,

> …God is the ultimate Power Source from which everything else emanates. God is the Supplier, the divine Power Utility, the ultimate Connection. Without Him, you'll always be unplugged and useless. But once you get hooked in to that Utility, the power will come on in your life and you'll begin to manifest new radiance beauty you've never known. And you'll become useful in a multiplicity of ways (p. 132).

Deion also discovered that,

Unless you have God in your life, and unless He gives you the capacity to put it in proper prospective, you will never find peace with money. First you've got to have peace with God, and then with yourself (pp. 109-116).

The Mathematics of Life

"My life experiences, on and off the court, helped me develop the mentality that I have. At the same time, it enabled me to make better decisions for the people around me and myself. I think that's the most important thing. Learning from your experiences, especially your mistakes. Not looking at your failures as something negative. Finding the positives in them. And knowing that through your failures you are going to develop a different mentality from it. Preparing yourself so you don't go through that again. And your approach gets a whole lot better each time around. It's a maturation process that everyone goes through if they allow themselves to and if they surround themselves with positive energy. I think that's the key. If you put yourself around the right people and positive energy, then good things happen to you. Believe me."

- Alonzo Mourning,
Professional basketball player

The principles that hold true in mathematics, hold true in life particularly in the areas of positive and negative influences. For example, the act of adding positive and negative numbers mathematically produces the same results as adding positive and negative people with positive and negative energies in your life. In math, most people know that adding two positive numbers together gives you a larger positive number, and adding two negative numbers together results in a larger negative number. Such is the case with life.

Adding positive people to positive situations always create better circumstances and adding negative people to negative situations always create worse circumstances. Another rule of mathematics (in the adding of positive and negative numbers) is that the outcome always assumes the sign of the larger number (i.e. -10+6=-4). Life follows suit again. However in the context of life, positive-thought or optimistic thinking at all times remains the bigger number. This phenomenon can be attributed to fact that optimism never allows negativity or pessimism to become so large that it dominates an individual's outlook on life. In order to prevent any situation from having a final detrimental or destructive result, successful individuals combine their positive-thinking with the positive-thinking of other people to keep from dwelling in negative thoughts or thinking the worst in any situation. People who have attained success have mastered the art of pitting potentially disastrous circumstances in two-on-one battles against their positive energy and the positive energies of people around them – battles negative situations can't win by themselves. So, master the only powers that you hold within your locus of control:

- Your ability to be positive,
- And your capacity to surround yourself with positive people.

These powers allow you to create good results whether a life situation is positive or negative. As Dr. Dennis Kimbro, author of the book *Think and Grow Rich: A Black Choice* states: "Though you may not be able to control all the circumstances that surface in your life, you are able however to control your response to those circumstances (p.27)."

So, What Does Being Positive Mean?

For those who are not sure what being positive means, let's make some points clear. First, start the process by recognizing that positivity is a two-tiered state of consciousness that begins with the capacity to continuously create optimistic viewpoints toward life. People in our society who develop and maintain optimistic outlooks in their day-to-day dealings are called optimists. Optimists search for the greater good or ultimate benefit in any given situation, making sure that negative or self-defeating thoughts/actions don't overpower them or bring them down. As a result of their persistent searches for good, they find outcomes that allow them to become empowered - inspiring those closest to them to search for the same in their lives. The second part to being positive combines an optimistic outlook with a sharing, loving, and community-building approach of intertwining your loved one's and family's interests into the fabric of your interests. African-Americans often describe this principle as "staying true" or "looking out" for the ones you love. Positive people "look out" for the people they care most about by staying in tune with their loved ones goals and aspirations and by making every attempt to ensure that their personal actions/beliefs don't bring harm to these individuals.

Note: My purpose in defining the positive state of consciousness is because I have witnessed people make the incorrect assumption that they have surrounded themselves with positive people just because the people they have associated themselves with are fun to be around or make them laugh or smile. Although smiles and laughter can be signs of a positive person, these character traits alone do not make them positive people.

Similar to this erroneous assumption is the reoccurring mistake made about the African, spotted hyena's laughter. People often assume that the hyena's laugh means that the animal is a happy or playful creature. After observing the animal in the wild, it doesn't take long to discover that the hyena's strange laugh is not an indicator of good will. Witnessing the animal tear into a wildebeest's hide or ravage the carcass of a slain antelope's body all while it continues to cackle brings forth the realization that the animal's laugh hides an agenda that's much more dangerous and sinister. Laughter and smiles in people can also hide agendas that carry ill intentions. So, don't get caught up. Always be careful of the company you keep and work to create and maintain relationships with positive people in your life.

Do not be discouraged if you have allowed negative situations, people or environments around you to create negative outcomes for you in the past. Learn to discover the positives that you can ascertain from these results. These positives are:

• Better knowledge. Powerful lessons can be learned from doing things wrong. Through making mistakes, you learn what not to do or how to do things better the next time around.

• Enhanced emotional and spiritual resilience. When you take on and conquer various challenges, you develop increased confidence in your ability to master tasks. You become stronger. It is only through managing yourself during difficult times that you develop strength.

• An improved ability to face personal faults, fears and bad decisions. This is called taking ownership or developing accountability for your actions. Analyzing the how's and why's of any situation that resulted in a negative outcome helps you gain better insight of your part in that outcome. You are given the opportunity to look at your strengths, weaknesses, likes/dislikes, wants and needs. Facing your personal faults and past decisions are difficult things to do - you may find yourself displeased with what you see. You may find the thought of what it would take to change these qualities even more disturbing. But, it is only through this kind of evolution that a person's growth reaches higher, more mature levels of development.

These three life lessons speak to the positive of self-improvement. After you experience a negative outcome, find time to exercise one or all of these lessons therefore making any situation a life-learned positive experience. In the end, it's up to you to exercise your power of control and put the positives into place that will produce goodness in your life.

The Masterpiece: Past, Present, You are the Future!

We Have The Power!

*"Regardless of what white America does or does not do,
the destiny of African Americans is in our hands."*

\- Robert Woodson

According to a 1998 United States Census Bureau study, income for the average African-American household has reached an all-time high of $25,000 – an increase of 16.8% over the last five years. In 1998, Black-buying power in America also reached a record high of $533 billion. In addition, the number of African-American owned businesses in all industries increased nearly 60 percent between the years 1987 and 1992. To further emphasize the depth of African-American progression, seventy percent of all African-Americans are high school graduates and twelve percent possess at least a Bachelor's degree or more, thereby making African-Americans more skilled and more educated than any other time in the history of America. Our influence has also reached the boardrooms of Fortune 500 companies across America where African-Americans are in a growing number of decision-making positions. No more are the days when we can blame our problems on other people. This time more than any other in our history represents the Golden Era of African-American prosperity.

Our time to lead has come. The days are gone for our mothers and fathers to take care of us. Their job is done. Now we are the mothers and fathers of a new generation of African-Americans in need of our strength, determination, will-power and faith. The Civil Rights Leaders of the 1960's have passed the baton and it is our responsibility to ensure that their legacy is preserved. Stand up, be strong and continue fighting for the values that made our society a better place in which to live, work and play. Values like humanity, peace, love, justice, family and brotherhood have been and will continue to be causes worthy of your tireless thoughts and efforts. Fill your communities, families and churches up like fountains after heavy spring showers with these 'truths' as we know and have experienced them to be. Remember that weak links are useless in our battle for good, so work diligently to strengthen yourself and those around you.

Realize that we have the power! We have the power to cure all of the economic ills found present in our communities today. We have the power! We have the power to cure all of the psychological as well as spiritual ills found in our homes, streets and prisons. We have the power! We have the power to cure all of the illnesses related to our physical, mental and emotional health. We have the power! We have the power to make our communities safer for our families to live, work, and play. We have the power to solve all of these problems. But, understand that these problems will only be solved when we learn that the answers to these issues lie within ourselves. The world is desperately seeking young brothers and sisters across America who are courageous enough to step up and meet these challenges. Know that our failure to do so contradicts everything in our lineage. This is our mission... This is our goal... This is our destiny... young, African Americans! Make it happen!!!

LIVE LIFE!

Special Thanks to:

My family for all their support: Mom, Dad, my wife – Monica, our children – Quincy Jr. and Savannah, my mother in law – Linda Lee, and my father in law Willie Lee (R.I.P.). I love you guys dearly. Without you, none of this would have been possible.

My friends and supporters: Sonia Murray (your patience and willingness to offer your time and insight was invaluable – I will never forget and am forever indebted), Steve "Six Fo'" Washington and family (thanks for "staying in the hole" and showing me by example how to stay patient and prayerful during tough times), My Crew: Kenny Phillips, Paul and Steve Miller, and Patrick Smith; Lang Whittaker, John Cleveland and family, Mike Weaver and family, "DJ Dock" Irving and family, The Tiger Woods Foundation Family (Leroy Richardson, Pete McDaniel, Marcus Williams, Greg Marshall, and Conan Sander) Mary Catherine-Bassett, Laura Ciocia, Tresa Sanders, Carl Rosenthal, Tony Phillips (I'll never forget that faithful day when you introduced me to Dr. Kimbro's first book, thanks!), Dexter Dean and family (you've showed me that with a great spirit, a great wife and a supportive family that success is possible no matter where you are), Greg Lyons and Barbara Pescosolido of No Limit Records; Ryan Cameron, Twana James, and The Hot 107.9 Family, The Georgia State University Computer Lab Team: Raj, Ken, Martin, Perry and Francois; Carleen Donovan, Aaron Goodwin, Sharmaine Webb, Fred Toczek, Brook Stevenson, Makeda Smith, Stephanie Patterson, Joanna Stokes, Carmen Green and Lisa Joseph at Sports Entertainment Solutions, Norm Horton, Chris Stark, Leslie Short, Dionne Wallace at State Farm Insurance, Patrick Yancey, Chris White at Absolute Boxing, The Atlanta Public School System, and Jamaica Carter and Casandra Butler at The New Deal Productions. Thanks!

My research and writing assistants: Jemima Yakah, Earlie Billups, Akbar Imhotep, and Sonya Tate. Thanks for bringing light when it seemed like nothing but darkness existed.

My mentors: Dr. Dennis Kimbro and Dr. Roosevelt Thomas, Jr. for their vision, courage and support that gave me inspiration and got me through. Thank you to all the participants in the book: Ayinde Jean-Baptiste and family (thank you for your patience and willingness to put up with all my calls), Mara Brock-Akil, Rev. Jamal Harrison-Bryant, Jermaine Dupri, Alan F. Daniels, Edward S. Brown, Komichel Johnson, Elise Durham, Master P, Niki Butler Mitchell, Ananda Lewis, Sharmell Sullivan, Tiffany Cochran, Angela M. Lewis, Malcolm Berkley, Keith Clinkscales, Alonzo Mourning, Kevin J. Clash, Daymond John, Michael Vick, Jessie Tuggle, Laila Ali, and John Singleton. Peace out to Imani Lemone (R.I.P.) and all others that made this book a reality. God bless!

Bibliography

1. Cooper, Henry. *Before Lift-Off: The Making of a Space Shuttle Crew.*
Baltimore: John Hopkins University Press. 1987.

2. Rothman, Milton A. *Discovering the Natural Laws: The Experimental Basis of Physics.*
New York: Dover Publications.1989.

3. National Aeronautics and Space Administration. *Astronaut Selection and Training.*
www.jsc.nasa.gov.

4. Allen, Frederick. *Secret Formula.* New York: HarperCollins, 1994.
ISBN 0-88730-672-1.

5. Gorman, John. *Classic Case of Formula Forethought?* Chicago Tribune. 14 July 1985 (p.C3).

6. Greising, David. *I'd Like the World to Buy a Coke.*
New York: John Wiley & Sons, 1998. ISBN 0-471-19408-5.

7. Pendergrast, Mark. *For God, Country, and Coca-Cola.*
New York: Charles Scribner's Sons, 1993. ISBN 0-684-19347-7.

8. Potts, Mark. *Coca-Cola: Pausing to Refresh Formula?*
Washington Post. 23 April 1985 (p. C1).

9. LLCoolJ and Karen Hunter. *I Make My Own Rules.*
New York: St. Martin's Press, 1997. ISBN 0-312-96731-4.

10. The Marriage Movement: *A Statement of Principles.*
www.marriagemovement.org.

11. Waite, Linda J. *Does Marriage Matter?* In Demography, Vol. 32, No. 4, November 1995.

12. Schoeni, Robert F. *Marital Status and Earnings in Developed Countries.*
Journal of Population Economics, Vol. 8, 1995.

13. Gray, Jeffrey S. *The Fall in Men's Return to Marriage: Declining
Productivity Effects or Changing Selection?*
The Journal of Human Resources, Vol. 32, No. 3, 1997.

14. Cornwell, Christopher and Peter Rupert. *Unobservable Individual Effects, Marriage and the
Earnings of Young Men.* Economic Inquiry, Vol. 35, April 1997.

15. Kimbro, Dennis and Napoleon Hill. *Think and Grow Rich: A Black Choice.*
New York: Ballantine Books. 1991. 135

16. Greene, Robert and Joost Elffers. *The 48 Laws of Power.* New York: Penguin USA. 1998.

17. Jordan, Michael and Mark Vancil. *For the Love of the Game.* New York: Crown Publishers. 1998.

18. Malkinson, Terrance. *Self-Actualization and Your Career.*
www.todaysengineer.org/careerfocus/mar02/shorts/worldbytes.html

19. Sanders, Deion and Jim Nelson Black. *Power, Money & Sex: HowSuccess
Almost Ruined My Life.* Nashville: Word Publishing.1998.

20. Maslow, A.H. (1968). *Toward a psychology of being (2nd ed.).* New York: Harper & Row.

LIVE LIFE!